Zonke
Jimmy T
Doone

The Great T
Roland Burton Hedley, Jr....the folks and the humor that got us through the seventies are back. Jog your memory and remember the "good old days" and Trudeau's grand old strip with

DOONESBURY TRIVIA: AN UNOFFICIAL FINAL EXAM

CRIB SHEET FOR BACK COVER

1. He cut himself on a beer can tab.
2. The fall of the Chinese government.
3. Three years.
4. Harvard.
5. Big Mac.
6. A polka dot tie.
7. Bernie.
8. By Mark's BMW motorcycle and Mike's sidecar, the Doonesbuggy.
9. "The fighting young priest who can talk to the young."
10. Unconditional Amnesty and Kent State.
11. WBBY.
12. "Last Lap" Larry got a "hip" notice from his draft board, had his girl friend break up with him, and graduated all in the same week.

DOONESBURY TRIVIA:

AN UNOFFICIAL FINAL EXAM

Jeffrey A. O'Hare

WARNER BOOKS

A Warner Communications Company

The comic strip "Doonesbury" is syndicated by the Universal Press Syndicate and has been published in book form by Holt, Rinehart and Winston under the auspices of Universal Press Syndicate.

The copyright to the Doonesbury comic strip is held by G. B. Trudeau. This book is not authorized by him, nor by the Universal Press Syndicate, nor by anyone connected with or authorized by either party.

WARNER BOOKS EDITION

Warner Books, Inc.
666 Fifth Avenue
New York, N.Y. 10103

A Warner Communications Company

Printed in the United States of America

First Printing: October, 1984

10 9 8 7 6 5 4 3 2 1

ALL MY LOVE AND THANKS GO TO
Ginny,
Ed and Ellie,
Adam and Sean,
Steve, Kevin and the RTS,
All those who believed in the quest,
of course, Brian,

And all the crew down at Walden Puddle.

Contents

Prelude   1
Doonesbury   4
College Days   7
Walden   11
The Great Trek   13
Reverend W. Scot Sloan   15
Mark Slackmeyer   17
Radio Personalities   20
The Slackmeyers   23
Politics   25
B.D.   28
Boopsie   31
Phred   33
Uncle Duke I   37
Honey   46
Zeke Brenner   48
Quotes I   50
Zonker Harris   51
Nate Harris   55
Plant Life   57
Tanning   59
Jimmy Thudpucker   61
A Doonesbury Special   63

Real People   65
Roland Burton Hedley, Jr.   66
Duane Delacourt   69
Events from the Headlines   71
Rick Redfern   74
Joanie Caucus Redfern   77
J.J.   81
The Kids Are All Right   83
Virginia Slade   85
Lacey and Dick Davenport   87
The Brother of M.J. Doonesbury   90
Rufus Jackson   91
Quotes II   93
Fin de Decade Party   94
Extras   95
Titles   98
Uncle Duke II   100
Doonesbury on Broadway   103
The Man Behind the Scenes   110
The Answers   113

Prelude

Students, you may now open your texts!

Suppose a cartoonist walked into your newspaper office with an idea for a new comic strip. The strip would be four boxes long, have straight-faced characters that spoke without word balloons, have no cute or funny animals, and sometimes the same picture would appear in each of the four boxes. If you were the editor, what would your reaction be? Would you print that cartoon? No way, right?

Well, you would've just turned down one of the funniest, most successful, most controversial strips to ever appear in print. In the past twelve years, no other comic has created the kinds of laughter, as well as the kinds of apoplexy, that "Doonesbury" has.

"Doonesbury" is in a class of political satire and conscientious awareness that very few strips ever reach. Al Capp and Walt Kelly were two of the front-runners in this genre, and probably the best known purveyors of its dubious charm. But it has come a long way since its innocent inception, oh so long ago. Now even the masters admit that Garry Trudeau's biting work has surpassed all others. Though many pretenders to the throne have adopted Trudeau's simplistic style, none have come close to his incisive, clear-cut imagery, and humor.

No one is safe from Trudeau's barbed ballpoint. Actors, presidents, sports stars, reporters, newspapers, television, trends, and friends all come under the heading of fair game. Yet none of the salvos launched in any direction are sent with malicious intent. Usually both sides of an issue would get equal time in this hallowed strip, and both would be shown to be equally absurd.

Part of what has helped to make "Doonesbury" so popular is that everyone who reads it can identify at least one of the people in the strip. Readers see themselves or people they actually know trapped in the absurdities that abound in the world as seen by Trudeau. Even the rich, the famous, and the powerful cannot escape the annoyances that attempt to thwart us all.

Conflict plays an important role in Doonesburian humor. But it's not the violent conflict of a Tom and Jerry battle. It is more the quiet conflict of differing realities. Generations don't fight over the gap, they just see it from different perspectives.

And seeing is all-important because images are what "Doonesbury" is principally about: images of how we view others, how others view us, and how we view ourselves. The conflict among the classic triumvirate is what makes us laugh at the poor souls who inhabit the Walden Puddle area.

Our stuffy defenses are broken down by that laughter, and our simple commonality is strengthened. The facades we've developed are gently stripped away and we are found to be vulnerable. Then comes the inner dialogue with which we reassure ourselves of our existences. These are all that protect us from the outside world, and yet even these defenses are laughed at, as if Trudeau wants to ask, "Hey! What difference does it all make anyway?"

After all these defenses and images are broken apart, it is the sameness in our humanity that we share with characters like Mark, Zonker, B.D., and especially Doonesbury, the man himself. This is the key to what has made the strip the success it is.

Of course, the outside world beyond our control has its point, too. When an image such as a magical spring moment in the dead of winter, or one as simple as the tearing down of a wall, can make us laugh, the man must be doing something right.

But then, like a sharp slap to our social consciousness, it

was all taken away. "Doonesbury" left the pages of our favorite papers to try and make a success of it on Broadway. We had nothing to grab onto to keep ourselves steady in the floundering sea of world news. For many months, we've been cut adrift, having to make due with lesser strips. But lo, a beacon now shines in the distance. As we near the end of Trudeau's vacation and his characters' growth period, we can rejoice for their pending return.

Let us take a few moments to review then. Let's look back on how the strip and each of its characters developed into the people they are now. Hopefully, there'll even be a little insight into our own collective psyches of the time that was. Maybe this test will even lead us to thoughts on what is to come in the "Doonesbury" of the future.

Be forewarned, though. This exam, like the twelve years we readers have shared with the strip, may prove too difficult. Still, let us reflect on these things that have gone before. After all, they didn't just happen in Walden. They happened to us all.

Doonesbury

The soft-spoken star of our show!!

1. Easy start: What is Doonesbury's full name?

2. Where is he from?

3. What was his teddy bear's name?

4. Who was his girl friend when he left for college?

5. Who were his next two girl friends? (This refers to girls he actually went out with, not the many he had fantasies about.)

6. What kind of girl would he like to marry?

7. Who are some of the other members of the Doonesbury family that have appeared or been mentioned in the strip?

8. How does his mother get by?

9. What was her aspiration as a child?

10. What is Doonesbury's favorite breakfast?

11. How does his brother serve it?

12. How does Doonesbury meet B.D.?

13. What nicknames does Mike give himself in college?

14. At college, how does Doonesbury spell "ignorance"?

15. During his early college days, whom did Mike tutor?

16. What was the name of the weekly column Doonesbury wrote for the campus newspaper?

17. Whom did Mike talk to about his early college difficulties?

18. During his encounter sessions, what dark secret does Mike reveal?

19. What politicians have Mike supported?

20. What does Doonesbury have to do to get sworn in as a worker on the McGovern campaign?

21. Which president was Mike called to the White House to meet?

22. Why didn't anyone but Doonesbury show up for John Anderson's speech?

23. Where does Mike drive Anderson?

24. Who is Danny Wattle?

25. Why does Doonesbury think John Mitchell did us a favor by dismissing the Kent State incident?

26. Who is Dave Popkin?

27. How does Doonesbury prepare for calling J.J.?

28. What spontaneous stuff does Mike like to use in a conversation?

29. What does Doonesbury call himself when describing his dating history?

30. Doonesbury had one uncle who made his living as a farmer. What did he grow?

31. How much did he make at it?

32. What was his favorite song?

33. Who was Uncle Henry?

34. How long had he been a commissioner?

35. Who turned him in?

36. What did the judge ask for when Henry confessed that he knew he had done wrong?

37. What sentence was given?

38. What day did Henry pick?

39. What information does Mike let slip that devastates Zonker?

College Days

A veritable potpourri of campus characters:

1. What college does the gang attend?

2. Who admits the kids to college?

3. How do some of the others think Mike was able to get into the school?

4. Which class?

5. Who is the president of the college?

6. Who is his secretary?

7. Who was Mike's lab partner?

8. What was the name of the starfish he was in love with?

9. Who was his girl friend after the fish?

10. Bernie forecast a day of respect and admiration for what minority group?

11. What was Bernie's rating on his werewolf formula?

12. What closely guarded childhood secret did Bernie reveal to Mike?

13. With money from sponsors, what did Bernie go in search of?

14. When Bernie experimented with Einstein's theory of relativistic speeds, where and when did he wind up?

15. What animal did Mike meet in lab class?

16. Who was the first Chinese exchange student?

17. Who was Nichole?

18. Who was the campus Black Panther?

19. What was his complaint about the racial balance of the football huddle?

20. Who was the waitress at the local campus diner?

21. What books was she reading when Mike came in to order?

22. Who was Skip Willis?

23. Who was Larry Drumburger?

24. What course does Professor Cavendish teach?

25. Who substitutes for him when he's out?

26. During one class, Bernie rigs a program that simulates a nuclear confrontation and allows each class member to

take the role of someone in the chain of command.
Whom did each of these want to be:

   B.D.?   Mark?   Zonker?

27. After every player drops out, who is left in charge of the U.S.?

28. When Bernie's congratulated on the realism of the final blowup of the world, what did he say he was up all the night before working on?

29. What was the name of the teaching assistant assigned to Henry Kissinger?

30. Why did Kissinger's students wear masks in class?

31. How did they refer to the then-leader of Iran?

32. Name the students who were in that class.

33. How did they get there?

34. Where did Mr. Perkins get most of the ideas for his totally uneducated questions?

35. Who was Charlie Green?

36. Who was the Vietnam vet who came to address the students?

37. Who is the most famous Russian country poet living?

38. What is the subject of the first poem he reads at the college?

39. Whom does Scot Sloan compare him to?

40. Who did President King address in the opening words to the 1970 graduating class?

41. How does he prepare for his address to the alumni committee?

42. What didn't they have in the campus newspaper?

43. Where did Mike and B.D. set out for on their first spring break?

44. What plane did they get on instead?

45. Mike once hosted a Fall Student Congress at his school. What demands were made by the following schools:

    a. Howard?
    b. Harvard?
    c. Stanford?
    d. Notre Dame?

46. What was the name of the delegate from the Connecticut Institute of Technology and how did he greet Mike?

47. As a result of the NYU delegate's motion, what was resolved at the Congress?

48. Why would Mike and Mark attend commencement exercises?

Walden

Definitely not your run-of-the-mill puddle!

1. How far from campus is Walden?

2. What does Walden look like?

3. Which of our cast members lived at Walden at any given time?

4. What were Bernie and Didi hoping the house would be?

5. Who is Walden's regular mailman?

6. What is one of the first meals served from Zonker's garden?

7. What name does Zonker give to one of Walden's squirrels?

8. Why was Joanie allowed to stay at the commune?

9. Why did B.D. think Mike really brought Joanie home?

10. How is Walden Puddle fed?

11. One time the puddle dried out and Bernie had to fix it. What did he use for his first attempt?

12.   What did he try next?

13.   Finally, he was able to remove the rock that blocked the spring. What did Zonker then have to do?

The Great Trek

In the early 1970s, like so many others who were searching for meaning in their lives, Mike and Mark set out to find America. Mike needed to get out of the house and Mark needed to get out of the garage. So began a new adventure.

1. Only Zonker was against their leaving. What did he ask them to do so he'd be sure they were all right on their search?

2. How were the pair going to travel?

3. As they set off, Mike quoted something his grandfather used to say before every family outing. What was it and what does it mean?

Below is a listing of the cities that the boys visited. Do you remember what happened in each of them?

4. Brooklyn?

5. Manhattan?

6. Philadelphia?

13

7. Washington, D.C.?

8. Miami?

9. Los Angeles?

10. San Francisco?

11. Las Vegas?

12. Denver?

13. In Philadelphia, how does Mark convince the mayor to let them stay?

14. What had the mayor mistaken them for?

15. What happens at Mark's lunch in D.C.?

16. What did they hope to see in Vegas?

17. When Mike asks to see the beautiful, exotic coed dancers, what does the bartender ask him?

Reverend W. Scot Sloan

Profiled in national magazines, this man of the cloth was prominent among those who almost got to see the Iranian hostages.

1. What did *Look* magazine call Scot Sloan?

2. What are some of his credits?

3. What is his specialty?

4. What religion is he?

5. What was the name of the coffeehouse he opened?

6. Where were the profits from it going?

7. According to Sloan, what was enough to drive a man to heavy dating?

8. When was his last date before asking Joanie out?

9. Where did he take Joanie on their first date?

10. How far did he and Joanie go?

11. What was Scot's parting remark to Joanie as she left him?

12. What does Sloan have that makes Joanie go out with him again?

13. How did Sloan celebrate the publication of his book?

14. During his trip to Iran, at what address were the hostages being kept?

15. After retiring, Scot set out to beat the Big A. What is the Big A?

16. What memory brought tears to Scot's eyes?

17. What was served at Scot's Walden Testimonial Dinner?

18. What paper does the Reverend go on to write?

19. With Mike's help, Scot buys a word processor. What soothing option did it come with?

20. What's the title of his first article for the paper?

21. What is the name of Sloan's dog?

22. His cat?

Mark Slackmeyer

For a guy who once had it out with Harry Reasoner, Mark has come a long way from radical to radio.

1. Mark has gone by two different nicknames. What were they?

2. What are his parents' names?

3. What jobs has Mark held?

4. Who fired him from the construction work?

5. What did Mark miss about that job?

6. What had Mark hoped to accomplish as a hard hat?

7. What was the year of the first class reunion Mark bartended for?

8. Why did Mark want to work in computers?

9. Where did he get that information?

10. What model computer was he assigned?

11. Upon returning to his home for the first time, what present does Mark give his father?

12. How does Mark dress for a holiday dinner at his grandmother's?

13. One day, Mark returns home from college and finds someone else's clothes all over his room. Why?

14. Mark's father once presented him with a bill for support over the years. How much was it for?

15. Why didn't his mother talk to his father about the bill?

16. What does Mark's cousin Bob do for a living?

17. Mark spent a lot of his early years as the campus revolutionary, often taking over President King's office. During one of these takeovers, Harry Reasoner interviewed Mark. What did Mark call Reasoner?

18. After Mark got ousted for being a radical on campus, what was his goal?

19. What news does Mark later give that makes his father faint?

20. Who was J. W. Snead?

21. What game does Mark like to play while traveling?

22. Who is Red Dog?

23. How long did the boycott last?

24. While in Washington on a peace march, what politician did Mark try to see?

25. What does Mark do to help Zonker keep up with the latest trends?

26. Why does Mark quit being a revolutionary and stop protesting?

Radio Personalities

If you don't do well answering this section, listeners, don't worry. You're still beautiful.

1. On what station does "Marvelous Mark" broadcast?

2. What number do you call to make requests?

3. On Mark's first show, whom did the guys down at Barney's Bar and Grill dedicate a song to?

4. What kind of music does Mark play?

5. What does that mean?

6. What are the songs "YMCA" and "Bad Girls" about?

7. Who does the Mellow Traffic Report?

8. Who sponsors it?

9. Where were these questions asked?:

   a. How many tons of bombs were dropped on Vietnam in November 1972?

   b. What has been the effect of the war on the moral fiber of the nation?

10. What are the answers to *a* and *b*?

11. Who dedicated the Watergate profile on John Dean?

12. On what show does Mark interview the famous folk?

All of the following have appeared on this show. Can you remember who each one is or what he does?

13. Miles Potash?

14. What did he write?

15. Ned Stax?

16. Bill Gallipoli?

17. Trevor Ferguson?

18. Dr. Ali Mahdavi?

19. Albert Schoenfeld?

20. Everett Wanamaker?

21. Ernie Riback?

Perhaps the most famous of all Mark's guests is Dr. Dan Asher, the Mellow Meister himself.

22. What award has Dan won?

23. Can you name any of the books Doctor Dan has written?

24. What do you need for Beginners' Mellow?

25. Translate William Blake's "The moon like a flower in heaven's high bower, with silent delight sits and smiles on the night" into Mellowspeak.

26. According to her lawyer, how does Jackie Onassis feel about working at Viking Press?

27. Whom did Mark interview in a live remote from Washington?

28. Who takes over for Mark when he can't be at the station?

The Slackmeyers

Mark's capitalist parents previously had to hide their wealth, but were finally able to come out in the Glory Years under Reagan.

1. Where did the Slackmeyers live?

2. What did Phil do for a living?

3. What did they do with the servants whenever Mark came home?

4. What kind of return did Phil want on his investment in his son's education?

5. How does Phil bid adieu as Mark leaves on the Great Trek?

6. Whom was Phil afraid that Mark would start dating?

7. What religion are the Slackmeyers?

8. What show did Phil watch in order to learn how to talk with Mark?

9. How did the Slackmeyers get into the Mayflower Club?

10. Why did Phil think blacks should be admitted to the club?

11. What was the first sign of the returning influence of wealth?

12. What was F.E.S.T.?

13. Why do the Slackmeyers hire illegal aliens?

14. To what government post was Phil appointed?

15. What did he plan to do with the extra income?

16. Why did Phil leave government for the private sector?

17. How was Phil able to write off his 1982 Superbowl tickets?

18. Whatever happened to the three-martini lunch?

19. What two companies did Phil try to take over?

20. Who got them instead?

21. How does Phil describe himself?

22. What was Phil's theory on how he got Mark as a son?

23. What vision passed before Phil's eyes when he had his heart attack?

Politics

What more need be said? In the wild world of government, no one is safe. Especially us.

1. After Russia and China, to what perilous country did Richard Nixon journey in order to "rebuild peaceful relations between the people of the United States and a people too long unrecognized"?

2. While there, where does Nixon place a wreath?

3. What did Nixon hope would be an outcome of this trip?

4. How did he sum up this trip?

5. What TV show did he interrupt to comment on his ninety-day freeze and pitch for reelection?

6. When Nixon left for Red China, whom did he leave in complete control of the country?

7. How does this person address the nation?

8. Which of his taped comments was Nixon afraid might be misinterpreted?

9. During the Senate Watergate hearings, a special bulletin interrupted the televised portion. What was that bulletin?

10. After Watergate, where was the only place it was safe for Nixon to give a major speech?

11. What did Nixon's California home become known as?

12. What song did they sing at John Dean's Watergate reunion?

13. What did Nixon's chief of staff, Alexander Haig, tell the investigating committee was his role in Watergate?

14. How did Trudeau show his feelings about the Watergate cover-up?

15. Kim, the Vietnamese refugee, imitated her favorite politician. Who was he?

16. What two great institutions did she say he would restore faith in?

17. When Sutton, the foreign policy expert, went to Carter's house, where was the presidential candidate?

18. What was the price of the lemonade Amy was selling?

19. Who was the first speaker at the Ray Donovan testimonial?

20. Who gave Rick Redfern his first big story?

21. What did she originally do?

22. What reason does Ventura's secretary use to get the congressman away from Tina and down to the floor to vote on his bill?

23. What's Ventura's excuse for missing the vote?

24. Where did Ventura meet Tina for their rendezvous?

25. Why did she turn the congressman in?

26. What was the headline about this story?

27. What does Tibbit read?

28. What fantasy excites Ventura during the reading?

29. How does Rick Redfern get the congressman to face the camera?

30. What was the last act of the Jeb Magruder concert?

31. When the U.S. makes a deal to send three black militants, four radical priests, and fifty draft-dodgers to Russia, what is it going to get in return?

32. What two TV spots did the Watergate conspirators come up with at the Dean reunion?

33. Who paid for John Y. Brown's political announcements?

34. What did J. Y. Brown think Affirmative Action was?

35. What two options was the Kennedy family working on to replace Camelot?

36. How long does it take a man to renounce everything he always stood for?

B.D.

Who says the world isn't all black and white?

1. In the strip, what does B.D. stand for?

2. What is B.D.'s mother's name?

3. What did his father do for a living?

4. What was his father's favorite TV show?

5. Where did B.D.'s parents come from?

6. What special training school did B.D. attend as a youngster?

7. Who was his partner there?

8. What summer camp does B.D. attend?

9. What does his mother send him at camp?

10. Where does B.D. get his sneakers?

11. During a campus discussion, B.D. points out that there are not 800 million people in China. What are there?

12. What does B.D. give the Chinese credit for?

13. Why did B.D. join the service?

14. What was his battle cry before leaving the country?

15. Who was the draftee who became B.D.'s partner in the army?

16. What was the first sight that greeted them as they flew into Vietnam?

17. Where were they stationed?

18. B.D.'s partner grew tired of always calling the enemy "Charlie." What alternatives did he offer?

19. What's the difference between a bombing raid and a protective-reaction strike?

20. In Nam, B.D. won a purple heart for a hand injury. How did it happen?

21. While on patrol, B.D. bumps into a jungle terrorist. Who is this man?

22. With what words does he greet B.D.?

23. Finally, after days of being lost in the jungle, B.D. decides to open a friendly discussion. What prompts this?

24. What amazing fact does B.D. discover about Communists?

25. What does B.D. call Phred in order to vent his anger?

26. What is Phred's reply?

27. Who autographed B.D.'s helmet?

28. Upon his return to the U.S., B.D. goes back to his first love, football. Who were the members of B.D.'s college team?

29. When B.D. asks for a sign to let him know if football is really "IT," what happens?

30. What number is on B.D.'s jersey?

31. What observation does B.D. make about his team in their huddle?

32. But how does he view himself?

33. What group does B.D. collect for in the huddle?

34. What is it about football that B.D. loves so much?

35. Which professional team is B.D.'s favorite?

36. Which is his next-favorite?

37. In what company did B.D. own stock?

38. Whom does B.D. date?

39. What was B.D.'s answer to the question, "What sort of look makes your man sit up and take note"?

40. According to B.D., what does the evil weed, marijuana, lead to?

41. What is B.D.'s view on Ronald Reagan?

Boopsie

A great, big, snowy, marshmallow, fluffy, pink, cotton-candy, and sunshine kind of person.

1. What is Boopsie's real name?

2. While B.D. was in Vietnam, Boopsie went out with one other person. Who was it?

3. After talking to Nichole in some of the early strips, what did Boopsie want to be?

4. What is her pet name for B.D.?

5. What does she read?

6. What is her forté?

7. For which magazine does she pose and for how much?

8. Who forbade her to pose?

9. What did she pose as?

10. Who took the pictures?

11. What was the title of the layout?

12. How long was she in Memphis and why was she there?

13.   Where did she stay?

14.   What sign did she get from the beyond?

15.   What did Boopsie want to send to Elvis's grave?

16.   What did the florist call it?

17.   What souvenir does Boopsie bring home to share with B.D.?

18.   What does B.D. say about people who "do" Elvis?

19.   What did Boopsie love about the McGovern campaign?

20.   On the phone, what did she address McGovern as?

21.   What was Boopsie's biggest concern about the bombing of Hanoi?

22.   What exercise program does Boopsie follow?

23.   What special clinics was Jane going to open?

24.   What needs?

Phred

Early in the series, B.D. made a decision to support his country by joining the police action in Vietnam. There, with a gun against his head, he met one of the pluckiest little enemies a man could ask for.

1. How does Phred introduce himself?

2. What's his claim to fame?

3. What is Phred's full name?

4. Where is he originally from?

5. Why was Phred a terrorist?

6. Where did he work out of?

7. Can you remember any examples of his style of terrorism?

8. Where does he shop for clothes?

9. Who are the proprietors?

10. What kind of music does Phred like?

11. What is his nickname for B.D.?

12. When Phred and B.D. get lost in the jungle, they stumble across a stolen cache of army supplies. What is it?

13. While sharing the supplies, what game do Phred and B.D. play?

14. What compliment does B.D. give to Phred?

15. When B.D. finally leaves Nam, how does Phred say good-bye?

16. What was Phred doing after the Americans left Vietnam?

17. What grant does Phred apply for and get?

18. After the war is over, Phred reports to General Teng. While Phred is there, Teng gets two phone calls. Whom are they from?

19. When hostilities in Vietnam are renewed, what team does Phred get traded to?

20. Why?

21. Before leaving for Laos, what gift does Phred get from his mother?

22. While traveling in Laos, Phred meets some destitute refugees who wish to share his hot rice dinner. How many refugees are there?

23. When Phred gets a vacation from the Pathet Lao, where does he go?

24. Phred comes up with a plan to make the U.S. take

responsibility for the Cambodian refugees. How does he get them to America?

25. What shipment was bumped for the refugees?

26. Who were the last refugees to find homes in Georgetown?

27. Who takes them?

28. During her testimony, how did the little old lady, Miss Loo, identify the plane that bombed her village?

29. How did Phred continue helping in Vietnam once all hostilities had ceased and he was released from the Pathet Lao?

30. When disciplining representatives of two squabbling factions, what does Phred tell them is all they have to lose?

31. Who was in Phred's class and who was supposed to be executed?

32. What team was more intense than Gilbert and Sullivan?

33. What was one of Marx's drawbacks?

34. What notable fact does Phred point out about Marx's wife?

35. Later, Phred is made Ambassador to the United Nations. What happened to his predecessor?

36. According to Mort the clothier, what would allow Phred to represent the interests of Vietnam in style?

37. Who is Phred's best friend in the U.N. and what country does he represent?

38. How are countries seated in the U.N.?

39. Who represented the Republic of Togo?

40. At the U.N., the struggle for peace goes on around the clock. Where 'bouts?

41. Who are the Third World All-Stars?

Uncle Duke I

The shadiest, loudest, craziest character of all. But boy, you gotta love this guy!

1. What is Duke's full name?

2. What other character is he almost related to?

3. Whom was he married to?

4. Where is he originally from?

5. What did his father do?

6. When did Duke move to Aspen and build his house?

7. What is Duke doing the very first time he's seen in the strip?

8. When was the first time Duke was called before a grand jury?

9. Who is Duke's next-door neighbor in Aspen?

10. Duke loved to take potshots at the singer. What was the bribe Duke accepted to stop sniping?

11. Who ran Duke's regular liquor store?

12.   What were the names of Duke's two Dobermans?

13.   How did he train them to stay off the furniture?

14.   What finally happened to them?

15.   Who was supposed to be the caretaker for Duke's estate?

16.   What happens when Duke has too much tequila and Coke?

17.   What drug did Duke take to prepare himself for addressing three hundred Young Republicans?

18.   What effects does it have?

19.   What kind of gun did he keep in his desk?

20.   What magazine did Duke work for?

21.   Who was the editor of the magazine?

22.   What was Duke's original position at the magazine?

23.   Duke once had to choose randomly from among six assignments. What did he wind up with?

24.   What post does Duke leave the magazine for?

25.   Who was his lieutenant governor there?

26.   What is the lieutenant governor's main reason for going?

27.   What was the name of Duke's administrative aide?

28.   What was the name of the aide's sister?

29. What was the aide almost named?

30. What caused his parents to decide?

31. What does the aide greet Duke with at the airport?

32. Duke had two points in his sweeping reform program. What were they?

33. How did the Samoans keep their volcano quiet?

34. How long had this been going on?

35. Who was the first one to go during Duke's regime?

36. What happened to her and why?

37. Who was Mopsy DeBeers?

38. What happened the night Nixon resigned?

39. When Samoa was hit with an earthquake, snow, cholera, floods, typhoons, and a volcanic eruption, Duke cabled the peace corps for help. What did they send?

40. What was one of the cabinet posts Duke established in Samoa?

41. What does Duke keep on hand as office supplies?

42. What does Duke do when he finds a seed in his orange juice?

43. What was Duke's first plan to gain U.S. Government notice for Samoa?

44. How did he finally get it?

45. What was the code name for the Marine rescue mission of these hostages?

46. On what islands did the Marines land in their search for Samoa?

47. What solution was Duke afraid of?

48. The final solution was for the U.S. to drop a punitive strike on Samoa. What did it hit?

49. When oil was discovered in Pago Pago Bay, what was the first sign of progress?

50. What bright future did Duke foresee for his people?

51. Who first comes to Duke to offer his congratulations about the oil discovery?

52. Whom does MacArthur report Duke to when he suspects the governor of taking a bribe?

53. What was #1 on the "comprehensive list of the many achievements inflicted on Samoa by his excellency, Governor Duke"?

54. How much does Duke tip MacArthur before stepping down as governor?

55. What going-away present do Mac and all 7,652 Samoan government employees give Duke as he leaves for China?

56. What legacy does Duke leave MacArthur?

57. What was Duke's obituary in *Rolling Stone?*

58. In what cool, calm way did Duke greet Wenner when the ex-governor returned to *Rolling Stone?*

59. Michelle is in charge of the mobile surveillance units, Annie coordinates paparazzi activities, and Lester is the inside man. Duke is placed in charge of these people. Who are they?

60. To what horrible place would Duke be sent if he screwed up this assignment?

61. Who is Duke's personal attorney?

62. Though a dedicated public servant whose personal finances are a matter of record, does Duke have a Swiss bank account?

63. Who calls Duke to ask him to be Ambassador to China?

64. Why was Duke chosen to replace Bush?

65. What was Duke's response when a reporter pointed out that the Chinese frown on all forms of excess?

66. What understanding does Duke have with President Ford?

67. What does Duke gamble on while in China?

68. Where did they have the best ones?

69. How much did Duke lose on Comrade Ting?

70. While in China, what Christmas presents does Duke get?

71. How does Duke practice with his pistol?

72. What are the dimensions of the Great Wall?

73. What did Duke send to Mao on February 17?

74. How did Duke feel to be in China, addressing the banquets?

75. What performance of the Peking Opera was Duke a guest at?

76. What was the overture?

77. Who wrote the play?

78. What happened to Duke's *Code of Ethics Manual* while he was in China?

79. What does Duke compare détente to?

80. Why are all labor leaders sensitive to the plight of the working class?

81. Upon his return to the U.S., what does Duke want to invest in?

82. What does he wind up buying?

83. Whom does he buy it from and what happens?

84. What supplies does Duke need for his lecture tour?

85. Before his first lecture, where does Duke hallucinate that he is?

86. What is the honorarium Duke accepts for the lecture?

87. How does he accept it?

88. Who is Edward B. Williams and why does he hire Duke?

89. Who was the answer to the Redskins' personnel problem?

90. What did he weigh?

91. What team did he first play for in the U.S.?

92. What team was he with before going to the Redskins?

93. How were they rewarding him?

94. What were some of his contract demands?

95. What college did he attend?

96. What was his worst game?

97. Who was Riley?

98. What does Duke see as every player's right?

99. How did Riley help?

100. During a home game, Eddie the linebacker gets speared in the ribs. What does Duke prescribe for him?

101. Eddie then goes berserk on the field. How does Duke calm him down?

102. Feeling it to be his civic duty, Riley then reports Duke to the papers. What reporter does he contact for a meeting?

103. What does Riley order during the interview?

104. How did Riley want to leave the restaurant after the meeting?

105. Who testifies on Duke's behalf during the press conference?

106. According to Duke's appointment book, where was he when Riley came to escort him to the greeting of the Chinese exchange students?

107. Upon retiring from the Redskins, why was Duke in Miami?

108. Where is he staying?

109. What is in his bathroom when he wakes up?

110. What is Duke's view on the U.S. Criminal Code?

111. Who was the National Riflemen's Association spokesman who wanted Duke's expert testimony on their behalf?

112. What was his offer?

113. Who was also testifying for the NRA?

114. During the hearings, the chairman asks if the NRA is against a simple requirement of serial numbers to aid police in identification. What does Duke see as a better alternative?

115. Who convinced Duke to go to Iran?

116. What was Duke supposed to do there?

117. What was it worth to Duke?

118. After he parachuted in by night, what was the code name of the operative Duke was supposed to meet?

119. What was Duke's code name?

120. What was Andrews' code name during this operation?

121. What was Duke's final offer on the rooftop in Iran?

Honey

When Duke was appointed Ambassador to China, he met up with a tasty Chinese dish who was as staid as he was weird. Whenever Duke was sure he was finally rid of her, an hour later she'd be back for more.

1. What is Honey's real name?

2. Whom does Honey think she looks like?

3. What album did Honey get Duke so he could test his new stereo?

4. What is the title of the hit single that was on the album?

5. For whom was she the interpreter before Duke?

6. Who was Mr. Zhang?

7. When Duke left China, what going-away present did he give Honey?

8. How did Honey finally get to the U.S.?

9. To whose class was she assigned?

10. How did she explain a sorority to her mother?

11. When she went looking for a sorority to join, what was one of Honey's major priorities?

12. In the U.S., what quickly becomes Honey's favorite food?

13. Why did Honey have to attend summer school?

14. Upon her arrival in the U.S., Honey called the State Department and found out that Duke was working with . . . whom?

15. What did Honey want Duke to show her on their first date in the nation's capital?

16. Why did Honey eventually return to China?

17. Who was the boyfriend she was going back to meet?

18. What was he doing now?

19. How many judges were there going to be at the trial?

20. How could the defense claim it was manslaughter?

21. What's the technicality in "State vs. the 5 Cockroaches"?

22. What is the Chinese dream?

Zeke Brenner

The caretaker Duke tried to take care of.

1. What is part of Zeke's religion?

2. What sign is he?

3. Whom is he dating when we find this out?

4. What book did he write?

5. Who published it?

6. What tense is it in?

7. Who actually wrote it?

8. What choices did he give Brenner?

9. What is "literary merit"?

10. Before Zeke takes his book on the talk-show circuit, what does Rick Redfern advise him to do?

11. What shows did Zeke appear on?

12. When Duke is missing in Iran, what does Zeke turn Duke's house into?

13. What was Zeke going to do with Duke's barn?

14. When Zeke had Duke declared dead, who attended the reading of the will?

15. What color ribbon does Zeke have waiting for Duke when he returns?

16. Who was the policeman who tried to arrest Duke for attempting to murder Zeke?

Quotes I

Who said what about what or whom?

1. "Human rights! Human rights! I'm sick to death of hearing about human rights! What do you want anyway—peace or human rights?"

2. "A cynic is someone who knows the price of everything and the value of nothing."

3. "I can't respect someone who respects someone who respects a sexist."

4. "His little band does not produce music. Rather, it emits a field of intensely unpleasant vibrations that can sterilize frogs at 200 yards."

5. "I mean I just want it to rhyme!"

6. "You encourage them breathers, they just keep calling back."

7. "Blacks are the wrong symbols for the 1970s."

8. "Those in search of the meaning of humane letters need go no further than Doonesbury."

Zonker Harris

If innocence were given form, it would be his.

1. What is Zonker's real first name?

2. Where is he from?

3. When he was growing up, who was his best friend and neighbor?

4. How did Zonker get to Disneyland?

5. How long was Zonker a sophomore?

6. After Roland Hedley's first report on student life, what was Zonker's claim to fame?

7. Whom did Zonker want invited as guests to the *Rolling Stone* party in his honor?

8. What personal papers does Zonker donate to the college?

9. How much were they worth?

10. How was Z. able to cut his school costs down to only $3400 a year?

11. What is one of Zonker's greatest fears?

12. To keep this from possibly happening, Zonker joined the Ginny Slade campaign as press liaison. Where was Press Officer Harris when *Newsweek* called for a story on the campaign?

13. Whom does Zonker take dibs on when canvassing for Slade?

14. How did Zonker become a war correspondent?

15. What new position did Z. contribute to his college football team?

16. What position did he regularly play?

17. What made Z. feel better about registering for the draft?

18. What is Zonker's favorite avocation?

19. Who are his closest friends?

20. What is the strongest profanity he's ever used?

21. What is his favorite expression?

22. Whom did Z. nominate at the '72 Republican Convention?

23. Whom did his mother want to run?

24. What did the delegation from Rhode Island want?

25. Where and when did Zonker's parents go to college?

26. At one point, Zonker's mom and dad had a fight that almost ended in divorce. What was the fight about?

27. How long had they been married when this happened?

28. Why was Z. not worried about the fight?

29. What are some of the jobs that Z. has held?

30. What annoying habit did Zonker have as a mailman?

31. When Z. is tending bar at a reunion, he forgets a certain drink recipe. What drink is the recipe for?

32. Z. then switched over to real bars. Who was his first customer in a real bar?

33. What does the gang at the bar give her for her birthday?

34. Why did Z. leave his post as lieutenant governor of Samoa?

35. Whom did Zonker have nightmares about?

36. While vacationing with Mike, Zonker is busted for possession of "mary-gee-wanna." When he is thrown in jail, who is his cellmate and what is that man in for?

37. What is the name of the dog who sniffs out the dreaded weed?

38. How much did Zonker have in his possession?

39. What happens to the district attorney's case?

40. Who did Zonker think John Travolta was?

41. Why hadn't Zonker liked discos?

42. At Studio 54, who came out to sign autographs for all those who couldn't get in?

43. Whom did Zonker want to be included with that group?

44. Who was Zonker's great uncle?

45. What was the last course that stood between Z. and the real world?

46. With Mike's assurances that there were no jobs out there, Z. arranges some interviews. What four companies does he go to see?

47. According to Z., what is a life well-spent?

48. At Christmas, what song does Zonker sing while the rest of the Walden crowd is singing "We Wish You a Merry Christmas"?

Nate Harris

One of the original Harrises and the first in a long line of wackos.

1. What qualifications did Nate have to be a minuteman?

2. Whom was Nate married to?

3. How did she want to help the cause?

4. Whom did she go to work for?

5. How long was her apprenticeship?

6. Who was John Hancock?

7. Where did these Harrises live?

8. Who was their neighbor?

9. Who was their neighbor's slave?

10. What state did the neighbor tell his slave they lived in?

11. How did Nate feel about the Declaration of Independence in regard to blacks?

12.   What unconventional tactic did the minutemen use when fighting the redcoats?

13.   How did the redcoats feel about it?

14.   What was Nate going to buy for Amy after the War for Independence?

15.   What did Nate plan to do with his new liberty once the Constitution was ratified?

Plant Life

Zonker, Walden's resident green thumb, attributes his success with plants to the fact that he talks to them. They, however, have something entirely different to say.

1. What did Zonker first attempt to grow at Walden?

2. What did Bernie recommend for harvesting it?

3. Each of Zonker's plants has a name and a unique personality. Name as many of these plants as you can, along with their types.

4. What did the plants serve at the party for Zonker's return from Samoa?

5. What happens in the spring?

6. What does Ed like to do?

7. What TV personality does Willy trust?

8. Where did Zonker take Patty?

9. Who gave the weather reports there?

10. What is "The Light and The Dark"?

11. Why did Rob want to become a tree?

12. What does Fred do in the fall?

13. Who was the head tulip at the White House?

14. How long had he been there?

15. Where was his post?

16. What did reporter Bob Schieffer say about him?

17. What does "E.T." mean to Zonker?

Tanning

It was either this or dentistry.

1. Which contest is the most prestigious in all of professional tanning?

2. What was the first technique Zonker used in trying to prepare for this event?

3. When that failed, Zonker was all set to return to California and enroll at a tanning clinic. Which one was he registered at and why?

4. Unfortunately, when he finally reached California, all the clinics were closed, thanks to . . . ?

5. What else did that man cut out?

6. Where did Zonker go to relieve his tanning woes?

7. What was one of the reasons Zonker wanted to study with George Hamilton?

8. What happens at Rancho Mirage?

9. Who gets disqualified from this event?

10. Who is Zonker's caddy, coach, and trainer?

11. What book do they look through in order to decide on which tan to go for?

12. Which tan do they decide on?

13. At the end of the contest, what was Zonker's combined score?

14. Does Zonker win any awards with a total like that?

15. Zonker's tanning made him a celebrity. He appeared on "Profiles on Parade" and "That's Amazing, America." Who were the hosts of "That's Amazing, America"?

16. Which is the only show that actually pays you to be tan?

17. What is Plough?

18. According to Zonker's press release, why is he going to give up tanning?

19. Who believes him?

20. Who is Nelson Cohn?

Jimmy Thudpucker

An overnight sensation by the time he was 19, Jimmy has thrilled millions with his music. If you happen to own the green-covered "Greatest Hits" album released after "A Doonesbury Special," hold on to it. You've got a real collector's item!

1. What is Jimmy's wife's name?

2. What special something is his wife going through when he writes a heartbreaking lyric for her?

3. When their first baby came, what were the four choices they had for names?

4. What book is Mrs. Thudpucker reading just before she goes into labor?

5. Who delivers the baby?

6. Where is Jimmy when he speaks to President Carter?

7. Where is his host?

8. Why does Jimmy always put one ''dues'' song—a dumb, self-pitying ballad—on every album?

9. What was the worst thing Jimmy could remember for a "dues" song?

10. What song did he write at Joanie Caucus's request?

11. What kind of song did Joanie want?

12. Who are the studio musicians who come in to work on it?

13. What does "Wah Wah" think of "Ginny's Song"?

14. What was on the flip side?

15. Who is Jimmy's producer?

16. What's the name of Jimmy's background singer?

17. When he retires, how does Jimmy collect stamps?

18. What countries was he working on?

19. About whom did he write the lyric "Might be obscure, this man with a cure . . . An other, but brother, he's pure"?

20. Jimmy gets upset with his wife when she forgets to record paying the phone bill. How much was left in their account to cover the check?

A Doonesbury Special

Lights! Camera! Action! After success in print, could TV be far behind?

1. Who produced and helped animate this special?

2. How were they first associated with Garry Trudeau?

3. What was Hubley's background in animation?

4. What event almost stopped the work on the special?

5. On what network did the special first air?

6. Who dies in the film?

7. Which inhabitants of Walden Commune don't appear in the special?

8. At Walden Day Care Center, which three kids are featured?

9. How does B.D. hurt his knee?

10. What is the Reverend Sloan doing in this special?

11.   Who plays the part of the Baby Jesus?

12.   What songs does Jimmy Thudpucker sing during the special?

Real People

A rose by any other name.... You may not have known it, but many of the Walden gang have famous alter egos. Do you know who each of these characters is modeled after?

1. Mark Slackmeyer?

2. Uncle Duke?

3. Lacey Davenport?

4. Rev. Scot Sloan?

5. B.D.?

6. Rick Redfern?

7. College President King?

8. James "Obscene Profits" Andrews?

Roland Burton Hedley, Junior

Look out, Uncle Walter!

1. What was Rollie's first assignment after being recalled from Saigon?

2. For what magazine?

3. What was the essay entitled when it was finished?

4. Whom did Rollie interview for it?

5. During Rollie's investigation of this subject, Zonker "lets slip" that there is casual sex at Walden. What does Mike say "casual" means?

6. What drugs was Zonker able to convince Roland most young Americans were taking?

7. What had Roland been covering for the Saigon Bureau?

8. What college did he attend?

9. What other magazine has he worked for?

10. Roland later returned to the campus for another "State

of the Student'' report, this time for ABC News. Whom did he interview this time?

11. What was the average sophomore's sex life like?

12. Who gave the dinner for Shahbanou Farah that Rollie covered?

13. What was Hedley's code name while traveling with the Carter press corps?

14. What does Rollie write before doing a TV story?

15. What was ''Cabin Fever: Footpaths To Glory''?

16. In that report, how did Sadat refer to the West Bank?

17. What did Begin call it?

18. How did Rollie sum up the Sinai?

19. Who was the focus on in ''Liberal Cult: Threat from the Left''?

20. For what show did Rollie file that report?

21. What was conservative columnist Dirk Dupont's answer when asked ''Who are these liberals''?

22. When Bart Svigals, congressman in hiding, was asked if he would overspend for Kennedy, what was his answer?

23. What has 700,000 words, 1,521 pages, and is the output of more than 30 months' work?

24. In his review ''Hype Henry! Memoirs on the Make,'' what does Rollie say about it?

25. When Hedley interviewed the new Vietnamese envoy to the U.N., Phred, what was the first question he asked?

26. According to Hedley's report, when did Reagan's Brain begin shrinking?

27. How about Carter's?

28. Who sponsored "The Search for Reagan's Brain"?

29. What was the title of Rollie's report on U.S. involvement in El Salvador?

30. While they are doing their laundry what does Rollie tell Joanie can possibly save her life when you're in the field?

31. Why does Rollie's boss continually send him to war zones?

32. Where does Rollie stay in Beirut?

33. When the PLO was offered evacuation, how many terrorists were counted?

34. How much were white flags?

35. What undercover work has Rollie done?

36. What one thing is always clear to R. Burton Hedley, Jr.?

Duane Delacourt

What it means doesn't matter. It's what you think it means that's important.

1. What is Duane's forté?

2. Who is his lady?

3. Who was the first man he worked for?

4. What was his post?

5. What agreement does he want before he'll take the post?

6. Who won when Duane was appointed?

7. What were some of his ideas?

8. What was a phone-a-thon?

At the Human Rights Banquet, a series of awards were given out. Can you remember who won for:

9. Most Improved Political Climate?

10. Most Improved Human Rights Climate·in a Developing Nation?

11. Most Improved Climate for Public Debate within an Authoritarian Political Regime?

12. Nation Whose Sense of Mission and High Moral Purpose Most Closely Resembled that of the United States?

13. Who accepted for them?

14. What was the most coveted award?

15. What was on these trophies?

16. What did Duane wear to the White House every day and what did he like to unwind in?

17. Why did Duane go on to be the symbols man for Jerry Brown?

18. What was his difficulty with Carter?

19. What was Brown's term for the world at large?

20. What foreign language does Duane study in order to accept this post?

21. What was Duane's code name for Brown?

22. What was Brown's opinion on any given subject?

23. How did the Delacourts synthesize their commitment to the California spirit of self-absorption?

24. Whom did Duane go to work for after leaving Brown?

25. What symbol does he come up with here?

Events from the Headlines

Extra! Extra! Read all about it! The following questions all deal with pertinent, up-to-the-minute strips that have appeared in "Doonesbury"! Extra! Extra!

1. Where did President Ford hold his early press conferences?

2. What was Ford's code name while skiing?

3. What was MAP?

4. Who was known as the Energy Czar?

5. What was he originally referred to as?

6. What did he use to grant energy allowances?

7. Who were the Rosenthals?

8. What were Kim's first words?

9. What did she say next?

10. Who were the three astronauts launched into space?

11. What government figure calls them with his congratulations?

12. How many people were killed by the maniacal "Son of Arnold and Mary Leiberman"?

13. Why?

14. How did the detectives finally catch the Son of Sam?

15. What happened in Rosewater, Indiana?

16. What did Harold Stassen tell Jimmy Carter made great stocking-stuffers?

17. How much did Carter have to spend in order to build a solid foundation for the future?

18. What was Billy Carter's answer when he found out nine U.S. senators were investigating his relationship with the Shah of Iran?

19. What was CONSCAM?

20. Who is Sidney Korshack?

21. According to the *Rolling Stone* interview, what did Cher say about Mr. Allman after their marriage?

22. What is Cher's favorite color?

23. Why did Cher name the kid Chastity?

24. What is the title of the section in *People* magazine that's devoted to stars in the process of divorce?

25. Of the ninety-odd guests on the Howard Cosell show, how many were introduced as "superstars"?

26. What were familiar sights on the streets at Patty Hearst's trial?

27. What was the title of the book Patty's boyfriend wrote about the trial and his ordeal?

28. What nicknames did Patty have for him?

29. How did Nancy Reagan describe the gun Ron had given her?

30. What did it shoot?

31. When Congress went after David Stockman, what did Reagan find in his bed?

32. How was Henry Kissinger tricked onto "This Is Your Life"?

33. Why did Marlo Thomas stop dating Kissinger?

34. Why did Kissinger try to conceal his role in the devastation of Cambodia?

35. What was Kissinger's code name for the Mayaguez Rescue?

Rick Redfern

A quiet, understated giant in the field of journalism.

1. What is Richard's middle name?

2. What was the first story he covered in "Doonesbury"?

3. What paper was he working for then?

4. Who was his photographer?

5. What paper did he work for before that?

6. What was Rick's position on that paper?

7. After the story in Question 2, what did Rick cover next?

8. Whose side was Rick on while covering this?

9. What does Joanie Caucus say that Rick misquotes in the *Post?*

10. Why does Rick promise to return to Joanie after the election?

11. What was in Rick's refrigerator before Joanie cleaned it?

12. To be with Joanie while she goes to law school, Rick had to work for Brenda Nicks at what magazine?

13. What was his agreement with Nicks?

14. What is PST?

15. What happens there at three o'clock?

16. What was the "classic of crying"?

17. What's it like waking up and realizing you're a contributing editor for *People* magazine according to Rick Redfern?

18. Before Rick could finally leave the magazine, what did he have to do?

19. For what reason does Rick condone Joanie's graduating from law school?

20. Upon returning to Washington, what did Rick and Joanie discover in his apartment?

21. Why was Rick chosen to cover President Carter's tour?

22. What was the nickname given to the carrier of the White House Press Corps?

23. Who gave Rick the scoop on drug abuse by the Washington Redskins?

24. What is the headline for Rick's exposé of Duke's drug dealings with the Redskins?

25. Who is David Halberstam?

26. What was the book to be called?

27.   What other books has he written?

28.   What after-shave does Rick wear for the interview?

29.   What did Rick compare Jerry Brown to?

30.   What was the title of the article Rick wrote on Brown's establishing a context for his campaign?

31.   When Rick was covering the Reagan campaign, from where was then-Governor Reagan getting his facts?

32.   Who was Rick's friend at the Environmental Protection Agency?

33.   Whom did he work for?

34.   What was he doing when Rick called?

35.   Among Rick's tags for the NYC Convention was a laminated clipping. Why was it there?

36.   What was the clipping about?

37.   What did Rick do with the notes from the wedding presents?

38.   What did he try to convince Joanie she had instead of being pregnant?

Joanie Caucus Redfern

A "fortyish" housewife gets picked up near Denver by two young men on a motorcycle. It's the beginning of a beautiful friendship.

1. When the boys picked her up, where was Joanie actually heading?

2. Whom was she married to?

3. What did he do to try to get her back?

4. How did Joanie react when he said, "My wife. I think I'll keep her"?

5. When they finally got a divorce, how did Joanie know her husband wasn't going to be too broken up about it?

6. When was Joanie born?

7. What is Joanie's mother's name?

8. On what date did Joanie make her last batch of "perfect fries"?

9. What is Joanie's Christmas specialty?

10. Where did Joanie get her first job after leaving home?

11. Joanie had a very tough time getting into law school, despite receiving a good grade on her law boards. What was that grade?

12. What four schools put Joanie on their waiting lists?

13. Which school did she finally attend?

14. Whom did she share an apartment with?

15. How much was the rent?

16. Whom did Joanie fall in love with at college?

17. How did they meet?

18. What happened?

19. What did Joanie think he meant?

20. What did he later go on to do?

21. Who was the class enthusiast?

22. Whose class were they all in together?

23. Whom did Joanie meet while working on Ginny Slade's campaign?

24. What birthday present did she later give him?

25. After graduating, whom did Joanie go to work for?

26. To what committee was she first assigned?

27. How much was Joanie getting paid as a staff lawyer?

28. Who later joined as another lawyer on the same committee?

29. How much was he initially making?

30. According to Lacey, did Joanie have any recourse toward justice?

31. What does Lacey keep forgetting about Joanie?

32. Who else keeps forgetting that?

33. Why was Woody making more money?

34. In the investigations, why was it important to screen out the innocent early on?

35. What is an Archie?

36. Joanie was originally going to be married on July 28 or 29, 1981, but Lacey advised against it. Why?

37. According to the announcements, whom was Joanie marrying?

38. According to the errata slips, what was to be his role at the wedding?

39. After all that, when and where did the wedding take place?

40. Reverend Sloan performed a lovely ceremony that was marred at only one point. Who spoke up when Sloan asked for any objections and what was the reason?

41. How long had Rick and Joanie been dating before they married?

42. When did Joanie get pregnant?

43.   Who led Joanie's natural-childbirth class?

44.   Joanie underwent an amniocentesis test that showed she
      would have what kind of child?

J.J.

A very cute date, who looks good even in overalls.

1. Who is J.J. and what do the initials stand for?

2. .When J.J. first enters the strip, how long has it been since she's seen her mother?

3. How old is she?

4. What grade school did she attend?

5. Why was she thrown out?

6. What is her favorite snack?

7. Whom is J.J. dating when she first appears?

8. Why did she leave him?

9. How did J.J. meet Mike?

10. What did J.J. assume Mike was?

11. What brought J.J. around to like Mike?

12. What did ex-boyfriend Zeke think Mike had that attracted J.J.?

13. Where does Mike take J.J. on their first date?

14. What is Consiglio's?

15. Whom does J.J. room with in college?

The Kids Are All Right

Out of the mouths of babes. Even the younger crowd like to get their licks in.

1. There were many cute kids at Walden Day Care Center. How many can you remember?

2. After Joanie started working at the center, what were the girls accused of acting like?

3. What kind of baby did Ellie's mom have?

4. What's wrong with Tommy?

5. Who is Chickadee McGee?

6. When the kids moved on to first grade, who was their teacher?

7. Who was the teacher that gave Howie "stirrings"?

8. What professional sportsperson did the kids idolize?

9. How many TV murders does the average American kid see by the time he's 14?

10. Why were Ellie and Sarah going to quit school?

11. Why did Howie say the ERA would never be ratified?

12. How did he suggest they try to reach women?

13. What do the kids give Joanie at her going-away party?

14. What was this note about: "My name is Bobby Matthews. I am 7 years old. Please don't hit me"?

15. Who was Malcolm Deveaux?

16. Who drove the bus?

17. What does Bobby call the black kid who takes his soda?

18. What does Bobby want while he's in the hospital?

19. Who was the National Guard sergeant in charge of the busing situation?

20. What was the name of the subpoena boy for the House Ethics Committee?

Virginia Slade

A young black woman decides to make a run for political office. Wouldn't it be wild if she actually won?

1. For what office does she campaign?

2. Why does she originally seek political office?

3. Whom was she running against?

4. At what time does she announce her candidacy?

5. When was she first supposed to announce it?

6. Why didn't Ginny want to resort to a mudslinging campaign?

7. Who was Ginny's press liaison?

8. What were his qualifications as a media person with TV background?

9. Who put out Ginny's position papers?

10. How much of the vote did Ginny sweep in the primary election?

11. According to Lacey Davenport, what would be best for Ginny after she conceded the election?

12. Who is Ginny's boyfriend?

13. How long had they been dating when Joanie moved in?

14. What was he always trying to do?

15. Even when he was visiting, what did he carry with him?

16. What job did he take in a department store?

17. What kind of car did he buy and for how much?

18. When he was recruiting for Ginny, what did he promise one part of her platform would be?

19. What ward did Ginny want him to canvass?

20. Why didn't he want to go there?

21. What costume did he wear in order to fit in?

22. Who was the landlord that was constantly evicting him?

23. Who was Ginny's landlady?

Lacey and Dick Davenport

The woman who beat Ginny for Congress and her live-in friend have had quite a charming life together. Remember the spring of '23?

1. To which political party does Lacey belong?

2. Since Lacey was rich to begin with, what did she plan to do with the extra money when she won the election?

3. How did she do in the primary she didn't even campaign for?

4. After being elected, what were Lacey's first two lobbies?

5. During the Ray Donovan investigations, Lacey was threatened by organized crime, even though it was the Senate and not Lacey's committee that was doing the investigating. The mob even sent her a bouquet of roses. What did the card say?

6. What was the party for Liz Taylor and John Warner called?

7. According to the invitation, who was the party for?

8. Was Dick going to this affair?

9. Before John was elected, how had the Warners planned to spend their fall?

10. How long had Dick and Lacey lived together before getting married?

11. What finally made them take the plunge?

12. Has Lacey ever looked at other men with lust?

13. What did Dick and Lacey do after graduating from college?

14. Where were Lacey and Dick first seen in "Doonesbury"?

15. How does Dick know George Gallup?

16. What color are Dick's eyes?

17. What branch of the service was Dick in?

18. What is Dick's hobby?

19. What bird put Dick in the 700 Club?

20. What is the 700 Club?

21. Who is Dick's bird-watching partner?

22. What happened to Iggy the pintail?

23. What was Dick's nickname in grammar school?

24. Do the Davenports know any gay people?

25. What was Dick's answer to the question "Why not Anderson"?

26. What does Lacey call the television media?

27. How did Dick feel about the Carter Cabinet?

28. According to Dick's research, did Reagan know about James Watt's appointment as Environmental Secretary?

29. What word really jumped out from Dick's petition calling for Watt's resignation?

30. At Dick's club, who signed his petition?

The Brother of M. J. Doonesbury

From medical school to the rock clubs of Berlin, Mike's brother is the epitome of searching for your own space in the American nightmare.

1. What is Mike's brother's name?

2. What college did he want to attend?

3. How many times did he write to the college?

4. When did he first apply?

5. What was his original aspiration?

6. What was his reason for this?

7. What was going to be the highlight of his career?

8. Who was his favorite movie star?

9. What did he later change his name to?

10. What is "Sal" short for?

11. What does he want to do with his life now?

Rufus Jackson

Always looking fine.

1. When Mike first comes to tutor this little denizen of the ghetto, what does Rufus call him?

2. If it wasn't because of his liberal guilt feelings, then why did Mike go down to the ghetto to teach?

3. What did Rufus want to change his name to?

4. What did he want to be when he grew up?

5. Where did he want to live then?

6. Who was Rufus' woman?

7. Who was his favorite character in the Bible?

8. What Christmas present does he call Mike about?

9. What role did Rufus play in Reverend Sloan's Christmas pageant?

10. What role did he want to play?

11. What butterfly did he try to catch for his collection?

12. What holiday did he invent in order to get out of working on his lessons?

13. When Mike tries to expose Rufus to the world outside the ghetto, he takes Rufus to a fancy restaurant. What does Rufus order there?

14. What was black after it was beautiful?

15. Why would Rufus not want to be white?

Quotes II

One more time! Identify these speakers.

1. "A serpent may be a hundred feet long, yet to kill it, only the head must be cut off."

2. "I like to think Hiroshima speaks for itself."

3. "We had a tough race. But happily the voters of the state of Virginia knew me and they knew what I stood for. Even when I myself wasn't sure."

4. "Do you realize, if it weren't for youthful dissent, this country would be a repressive police state haunted by pigs, fascists, gargoyles, and SST's?"

5. "There are only three major vehicles to keep us informed as to what is going on in Washington—the electronic media, the print media, and 'Doonesbury,' and not necessarily in that order."

6. "I don't think we should sit placidly by and let the gnomes of the world run over us without expressing indignation."

7. "It's not only the best comic strip but the best satire to come along in a long time."

8. "There is great disorder under heaven and the situation is excellent."

Fin de Decade Party

The toast said it all.

1. Whom does Mike come to the party as?

2. Whom does Mark come as?

3. How were the invitations given out?

4. Who topples at the party?

5. Whom do B.D. and friends come as?

6. Why does Zonker say to let them in?

7. Who was the bouncer at the party?

8. What were the major cultural contributions of the 1970s?

9. How did Mike and Zonker toast the end of the '70s?

Extras

It's the little things that make life interesting. This section contains all sorts of items that have appeared in "Doonesbury" but don't readily fit into any of the categories we've explored so far.

1. What sure beats working?

2. Where does that midnight train go?

3. What is Zieberts?

4. What happens there?

5. Is there really a Zonker Harris Beach?

6. What did the Prime Minister of Canada do when faced with nationwide campus disorder?

7. Who was the draft-dodger who took advantage of Jerry Ford's amnesty program?

8. What was the name of his valet?

9. Where were the proceeds from "Economy '74"—President Ford's domestic summit—going?

10. For what was Jerry Brown thankful to the Jesuits?

11. Though he had no answers to America's problems, why did Brown feel that people should vote for him for the presidency?

12. Of what was Paul Revere most proud?

13. During the Watergate hearings, the defense moved that all charges against Haldeman and Ehrlichman be dismissed and that they each be granted $60,000 pensions. What reason did the defense give?

14. What was the name of the "jiggle" show Freddy Silverman supervised at NBC?

15. What were the two policies that Silverman was going to use in order to save NBC?

16. Whom did Silverman want to cast in the roles of Begin and Sadat?

17. During the Koreagate scandal, Mark went to Washington, D.C., to interview Lacey Davenport. While there, Mark put a coupon in the papers for all his loyal listeners. Whom was that coupon addressed to?

18. How was it signed?

19. Who underwrote the entire cost of the Phyllis George-John Brown wedding?

20. In Iran, what do bearded holy men have for breakfast?

21. What does "Allahu Akbar" mean in Iranian?

22. What request did Prince Sihanouk make of Henry Kissinger that fully explains Kissinger's involvement in Vietnam?

23. What caused the 1974 recession?

24. What is the name of Jim Andrews' wife?

25. What lurks behind every blue collar?

Titles

The following are all titles of books that help to compile the Doonesbury saga. To what or whom do each of the following refer?

1. *A Tad Overweight, but Violet Eyes To Die For*

2. *Wouldn't a Gremlin Have Been More Sensible?*

3. *What Do We Have for the Witnesses, Johnnie?*

4. *As the Kid Goes for Broke*

5. *He's Never Heard of You, Either*

What are the titles of the books to which each of the following refer?

6. Kirby's comment as a butterfly lands on B.D.'s nose in Vietnam.

7. The Redskin money Duke paid out for Lava Lava Lenny.

8. Mark's unbiased radio commentary on John Mitchell's involvement with Watergate.

9. Duke's comment to Sid Kibitz as they sat in a Jacuzzi.

10. Nate Harris to his wife, Amy, late one night.

11. Who wrote the introduction to *Doonesbury's Greatest Hits?*

12. Who is quoted in the opening pages of the *Doonesbury Chronicles?*

13. Whom does Trudeau quote at the end of his preface to the *Doonesbury Chronicles?*

14. To whom is *The People's Doonesbury* dedicated?

Uncle Duke II

Though presumed dead, strange things keep happening to poor Duke.

1. While going through Duke's private papers, what did Zonker come up with?

2. How long had the Internal Revenue Service been after Duke?

3. Whom does Duke leave his entire estate to?

4. Duke was the fifty-third hostage released by the Iranians. What was their name for him?

5. Who were his captors?

6. What horrors did Duke undergo as a prisoner?

7. How much more in Iranian assets did the U.S. have to unfreeze in order to get Duke released?

8. In the hospital, after being released, Duke suffers from Stockholm Syndrome. What is Stockholm Syndrome?

9. What benefit does Duke receive as he's leaving the hospital?

10. Unfortunately, upon Duke's return to the U.S., his entire estate was gone, having either been burned, stolen, or sold. Who was responsible?

11. Being the level-headed thinker he is, what was Duke's reaction?

12. What was the first job Duke took while on the run for attempting to murder Brenner?

13. While Duke is on the lam, what bag lady does he meet?

14. What film project do they get involved in?

15. What is Duke's title for it?

16. Who is Duke's agent in Tinseltown?

17. Whom did the agent want to get to play the role of the young John DeLorean?

18. How does Duke plan to make money to support this project?

19. Later, Duke decides to buy a boat and start his own business. What kind of boat is it?

20. Whom was he buying it from and for how much?

21. What business does Duke open with the boat?

22. What was Honey's position here?

23. Who is Duke's first customer and what was the job?

24. How much does Honey charge him?

25. Whom did Duke meet instead?

26. What is the next job that comes up?

27. What happens here?

28. How does Honey try to console Duke?

29. Who was the only passenger left?

30. What happens to him?

31. What finally happens to the boat?

32. What animal do they meet there?

33. Where did the animal learn to speak?

34. Duke built a fortress to keep himself and Honey safe from cannibals and savages. What was the only thing he forgot to include?

35. Where were they actually shipwrecked?

36. Honey claimed the island for China. What happened to the mineral rights?

37. Who finally rescues Honey and Duke?

Doonesbury on Broadway

New Lights! No Cameras! All New Action! After TV, the gang has moved to the live stage of Broadway. Can a movie be far behind? The play is actually the piece that will bring the Doonesbury crowd up to date for their return engagement with the world. Hope you're ready for it!

Be advised: All questions below pertain to the play and to the play only!

ACT I

1. What are the two major events that are occurring to our heroes in the play?

2. Which of the comic-strip characters are used in the play?

3. What class is the group actually graduating with?

4. What did the gang forget to do while they were college students?

5. Who was the only one to actually be graduating with a profession?

6. What was that profession?

7. For what team?

8.   What were Mike's plans for after graduation?

9.   Where is Uncle Duke when we first see him?

10. What defense does Duke give?

11. Whom does Duke dedicate his plea to?

12. Who gets Duke off lightly?

13. What term does Duke use for her testimony on his behalf?

14. What is Duke's sentence?

15. What property does he buy for the center?

16. Who is Walden Commune's landlady?

17. Which of Zonker's plants have speaking roles?

18. What do they help him with?

19. What do Boopsie's parents think she's going to do after graduation?

20. Why does Boopsie like the Jane Fonda exercise program?

21. What is cheerleading a stepping-stone to?

22. How does B.D. feel about the Gender Gap?

23. Why didn't the ERA get passed?

24. What is Joanie's son's name?

25. What is J.J.'s comment on the women's rights movement?

26. What number do you call to make requests on WBBY? (Remember, this is according to the play.)

27. How does Roland refer to Cronkite, Chancellor, and Arafat?

28. Who is Rollie's Nicaraguan makeup man?

29. What big thing does Mike want to ask J.J.?

30. What memorable meal does Mike cook?

31. What ends Act I?

ACT II

32. What sound opens Act II?

33. What does Honey wear during construction?

34. When faced with possible legal action, what does Duke tell Joanie he has for breakfast?

35. What does he really usually have?

36. What is the only thing Duke wants to know about the restraining order placed against his construction?

37. What kind of "hardware" is Duke carrying?

38. What was Duke really going to do with Walden?

39. What position does he offer Zonker?

40. What is the high point of the second act?

41. After coming through the wall, what hallucinations does Duke see?

42. Who is the least concerned about leaving Walden?

43. Who is his agent?

44. What team does B.D. get traded to?

45. What does he get traded for?

46. What TV show does he like to watch with Boopsie?

47. What does B.D. like for breakfast?

48. If Boopsie followed B.D. to his new team, what squad would she be cheering on?

49. What is the name of the singing group formed by Boopsie, Mike, Mark, and Zonker?

50. What does J.J. do when left alone with her brother?

51. What does J.J. tell Mike when she finds out that he's never had sex before?

52. What offer comes through for Mark just before graduation?

53. What is Mark's middle name?

54. How do Boopsie and B.D. get to the graduation ceremony?

55. With what honor does Mike graduate?

56. What does Mark have to say about this?

57. What motto is written over the top of the school?

58. What happens to Zonker when they actually hand him a diploma?

BACKSTAGE
59. Who wrote the book and lyrics for the play?

60. Who wrote the music?

61. What are some of her other credits?

What are each of these songs about?

62. "Just One Night"?

63. "Guilty"?

64. "I Can Have It All"?

65. "Get Together"?

66. "Baby Boom Boogie Boy"?

67. "Just A House"?

68. "Complicated Man"?

69. "Real Estate"?

70. "Mother"?

71. "It's The Right Time To Be Rich"?

72. What other songs appeared in the final Broadway production?

Listed below are the actors that appeared in the play. Can you figure out what roles they portrayed?

73. Reathel Bean?

74. Albert Macklin?

75. Gary Beach?

76. Lauren Tom?

77. Ralph Bruneau?

78. Kate Burton?

79. Mark Linn-Baker?

80. Keith Szarabajka?

81. Laura Dean?

82. Barbara Andres?

83. At what theatre did the play run in New York City?

84. At what theatre did the play run in Boston?

85. How long did the play run in New York?

86. What new character was added to the play after Boston but before it went to Broadway?

87. What other things were added?

88. What things were taken out?

89. What team did B.D. originally get traded to in the Boston production?

90. Who played Jeffrey the baby in the play?

The Man Behind the Scenes

Behind every great character in "Doonesbury" is a very private individual known as Garry Trudeau, who hates interviews and likes to keep to himself. The following questions are based on the facts as they are known. However, their validity is at best questionable. Trudeau can be a very tricky person.

1. What is Trudeau's full name?

2. Where and when was he born?

3. Does he have any siblings?

4. To whom is he married?

5. Do they have any children?

6. What does he like to eat?

7. When Trudeau was young, what was his favorite comic strip?

8. Has he ever appeared on a TV game show?

9. What college did he attend?

10. How long was he there?

11. In what area is the degree he graduated with?

12. What other degrees does Trudeau hold?

13. What awards did *The Doonesbury Special* receive?

14. What award did Trudeau win for "Doonesbury" in 1975?

15. What did Trudeau do after receiving this award?

16. When and where did Trudeau's cartoon series first appear?

17. What was the original title of "Doonesbury"?

18. Who convinced Trudeau to syndicate "Doonesbury"?

19. When was the last date of publication before Trudeau took his leave of absence?

20. At that time, how many papers were carrying "Doonesbury"?

21. How many strips are presented in *The Doonesbury Chronicles?*

22. Have any of the "Doonesbury" characters been licensed or used as symbols?

23. Where is Trudeau's graphics studio located?

Many of the more controversial strips have been censored, deleted, or moved to extremely strange places. Below are questions pertaining to this annoying problem.

24. What strips did the New York *Daily News* refuse to carry?

25. How about the Los Angeles *Times?*

26. Or the Washington *Post?*

27. What do these newspapers have in common: *Deseret News, Newsday,* San Bernadino *Sun-Telegram,* Columbus *Republic,* Daytona Beach *News Journal,* Albany *Knickerbocker?*

28. What other "Doonesbury" series got banned?

29. How far will Trudeau go to insure his privacy?

30. What archaeological dig was Trudeau part of?

31. How does Trudeau know former NYC mayor John Lindsay?

32. Who is Nicholas Von Hoffman?

33. What did he and Trudeau write?

34. With whom has Trudeau compared himself?

THE
ANSWERS

Doonesbury

1. Michael James.

2. Tulsa, Oklahoma.

3. Ralph.

4. Elaine.

5. Lisa and Lily.

6. A girl who looks, talks, acts, and cooks like his mother.

7. Mike's mom, dad, grandmother, two uncles, a cousin, his brother, and once there was even mention of a sister!

8. She runs a feed store.

9. To be chairman of General Motors.

10. Scrambled eggs and bacon.

11. In a glass.

12. They were chosen by a computer to be college roomies.

13. "Mike The Man" and "Mike The Mix."

14. F-O-O-T-B-A-L-L S-C-H-O-L-A-R-S-H-I-P (in reference to his roommate, B.D.).

15. Rufus Jackson.

16. "Landscapes."

17. His bathroom mirror.

18. That as a child, he told his secrets to his teddy bear.

19. George McGovern and John Anderson, though not on the same ticket.

20. He has to raise his right hand and repeat "Come home, America" three times.

21. Richard M. Nixon.

22. Due to poor scheduling. It was on a Monday night when there was a basketball game against Columbia and an Annette Funicello Film Festival.

23. To Concord, New Hampshire, where Mike is recruited to drum up support for him.

24. Someone who reads Anderson's pamphlets and quits his job to work along with Mike.

25. Because they could now concentrate on fresher, more recent tragedies.

26. Mike's cousin and one of only three people in all of Los Angeles who have never been profiled in *People* magazine.

27. By making notes on 3 × 5 cards.

28. Baseball scores, quips, stuff from the news—just like Johnny Carson.

29. The master of the emotional belly flop.

30. Nothing.

31. $175,000, thanks to the government.

32. "My country, 'tis of thee / Sweet land of subsidy..."

33. Mike's uncle who was a county commissioner found to have been taking kickbacks from some lumber suppliers.

34. Fifteen years.

35. Mabel Travis.

36. His wrist.

37. Henry had to work one day a week on the county-road crew until they finished the highway that goes up past Ed Turner's place.

38. Monday.

39. There is no Santa Claus.

College Days

1. Though it's never been exactly mentioned, all evidence points to Yale.

2. Alan, the Amazing Admissions Officer.

3. Because his father was an alumnus.

4. 1946.

5. President King.

6. Betty.

7. Bernie.

8. Doris.

9. Didi, who helped pick out Walden and once snuck into ROTC camp to be with Bernie.

10. Werewolves.

11. 78, because the hair was a little coarse and the ears a little small.

12. When he was 4, he ate an entire outboard motor.

13. The Loch Ness Monster.

14. Buffalo, 1981. (The strip ran in 1979.)

15. Leonard, the talking frog.

16. Chou Fu Ling.

17. The campus feminist.

18. Calvin.

19. That only nine percent of the football huddle was black.

20. Anastasia.

21. Aristophane's *Lysistrata* and Malraux's *Man's Fate*.

22. A freshman at 26 because he had been a P.O.W. in Vietnam. He appeared on Mark's radio show.

23. "Last Lap" Larry got a hip notice from his draft board, had his girl friend break up with him, and graduated all in the same week.

24. Intro to Computer Science.

25. Bernie.

26. Alexander Haig, George Bush, The Mad B-52 Pilot.

27. James Watt.

28. Getting the little houses to blow down.

29. Dan Doheny.

30.   To show solidarity with the repressed people of Iran.

31.   The Shah-Na-Na.

32.   Barney Perkins, Mr. Weinberger, and, later on, Honey.

33.   They were all hand-picked.

34.   From books, mostly.

35.   The hippie professor who taught Consciousness 10-A and part-time sidewalk guru.

36.   John Kerry.

37.   Yuri Yetsky.

38.   Newark Airport.

39.   Rod McKuen.

40.   The students who trashed his office the night before.

41.   By screaming "The alumni are a royal pain in the neck!" into his bathroom mirror.

42.   A comics page.

43.   Fort Lauderdale.

44.   A flight to Cleveland.

45.   a. Howard: End racism.
       b. Harvard: End the war.
       c. Stanford: Restructure academic priorities.
       d. Notre Dame: More football games.

46.   Walter. ''Bleep. Null Set. Roger. Bleep, Bleep.''

47.   War is bad.

48.   They were free.

Walden

1. Approximately one-half mile.

2. A big ol' country house with 12 rooms, a porch, and forty acres of land.

3. Mike, Mark, Joanie, J.J., Zonker, Bernie, Nichole, Boopsie, B.D.

4. A ranch house with aluminum siding.

5. Ralph.

6. Wheat and macro-chaotic salad.

7. Leslie.

8. The "Ayes" voted her in.

9. For a little of the "old Mrs. Robinson."

10. Through a small underground stream.

11. Explosives.

12. Running a hose out from the house.

13.   Restock the pond, replant the lily pads, round up some
      replacement frogs, and convince the local ducks this
      would never happen again.

The Great Trek

1. "Call me when you get there."

2. With Mark's BMW motorcycle and Mike's sidecar, the Doonesbuggy.

3. "Cherchez les femmes!" (Which means," Keep an eye peeled for broads.")

4. Mike wanted to see the Dodgers play.

5. The boys and a taxi driver went to see the Rockettes.

6. They were met by the mayor, who ordered them out of town.

7. Mark took Kissinger to McDonald's and wound up with Henry's briefcase.

8. They met up with Zonker at the Republican Convention.

9. They got lost in the smog.

10. Mike goes looking for street people.

11. They gamble with Necco wafers.

12. They pick up Joanie Caucus.

13. By saying that he's a fellow Italian.

14. A hippie or a Negro or something.

15. Kissinger has Mark drink his chocolate shake in order to check for poison.

16. All sorts of depravity, vulgarity, lasciviousness, drunken euphoria, and wild physical animal abandon.

17. "Are you a college man?"

Reverend W. Scot Sloan

1. "The fighting young priest who can talk to the young."

2. Birmingham, Selma, Washington '67, Chicago '68 . . .

3. Setting up a dialogue.

4. Episcopalian.

5. The Exit, the coffeehouse where people can relate.

6. To wipe out poverty, hunger, hate, war, frustration, and inadequate housing.

7. Richard Nixon.

8. 1953.

9. To vespers.

10. They held hands.

11. "Your loss, Toots!"

12. Tickets to the Jeb Magruder concert.

13. With a sixties costume party.

14. 45 Death-to-Carter Avenue.

15.   Apartheid in South Africa.

16.   Memories of tear gas.

17.   Memorial cheeseburgers.

18.   A nuclear-freeze peace newsletter.

19.   A mellowspeak disc.

20.   "A Meditation On Deterrence."

21.   Unconditional Amnesty.

22.   Kent State.

Mark Slackmeyer

1. Marvelous Mark and Megaphone Mark.

2. Phil and Marilou.

3. He worked in Phil's brokerage firm for a bit, tried to be a computer-terminal operator, and worked as a hard hat (as well as being an ace radio jock).

4. The mayor during some cutbacks.

5. Being beaten up every morning.

6. To bring the word about a new revolution, a beautiful student-worker alliance.

7. 1943.

8. To earn $7,000, impress his friends, and meet girls.

9. From inside a matchbook.

10. A PDP-112.

11. The hair he just had sheared from his head.

12. In tight pants, boots, flowered shirt, and Mickey Mouse ears.

13. His parents rented his room.

14. $65,251.13   2 yrs. college   @4500. per yr.
                  4 yrs. secondary   @3500. per yr.
                  8 yrs. primary   @3380. per yr.
                  1 yr. nursery   @2135.
                  3 yrs. summer camp   @ 700. per yr.
                 19 yrs. clothing   @2710.
                         food   7345.53
                         presents   920.60

15. She was getting thirty percent of the take.

16. He's an undercover agent for the FBI.

17. A great gross, liberal establishment media freak.

18. To become an outside agitator at Cambridge.

19. He makes the Dean's List.

20. A trucker that Mark assists in organizing a national boycott.

21. GHOST.

22. One of the toughest, meanest, ugliest, most powerful trucking leaders ever to pilot a heavy rig. He also happens to be J. W. Snead's Cousin Ernie from Cleveland.

23. Fifteen minutes.

24. Hubert H. Humphrey.

25. He underlines *Time* magazine.

26. His attitude was changed after Watergate showed the government was unresponsive.

Radio Personalities

1. WBBY.

2. 331-9100.

3. The memory of Bertrand Russell.

4. Mellow sounds for your natural life-style.

5. Soft rock for white college graduates in their late twenties.

6. One is about meeting adolescent homosexuals in a public gymnasium and the other is a celebration of prostitution.

7. Bob Hallohan.

8. Linda Ronstadt Signature Model Roller Skates.

9. On WBBY's "Vietnam Quick Quiz."

10. a. 93,470 tons
    b. The effect has been a deterioration of spiritual priorities.

11. Dedicated from Donna to Joey.

12. "Profiles on Parade."

13. Masochistic jogger whose joy in life has been to travel this great land of ours turning people on to the sweet pain of jogging.

14. *Jogger Agonistes.*

15. Made a $25 million deal with Robert Stigwood that included a TV series, spinoffs, a major movie, sequels, remakes, posters, novelizations, and records. However, no one was sure what he did.

16. Famous fashion designer who said Mrs. Reagan borrows all of her fancy clothes.

17. Runner who took just over forty-one days to finish the NYC marathon.

18. Speaker from the Iranian Revolutionary Council, who comes on while he is at his class reunion.

19. Wrote *Future Schlock,* about media trends in the 1980s.

20. Man who books all of President Reagan's vacations.

21. Resident of Bedford-Stuyvesant and survivor of the last summer blackout.

22. A fellowship to the California Institute for the Mellow.

23. The titles:
    Mellow: How To Get It
    Winning Through Mellow
    Mellowspeak
    The Mellow Mortgage
    The Mellow Parent: Sharing Your Space With Dependents

24. A good ten-speed.

25. "Oh, wow. Look at the moon."

26. It means more to her than all the tea in Greece.

27. Lacey Davenport.

28. Zonker (and on occasion Mike).

The Slackmeyers

1. They first lived in New Jersey and then moved to Forest Hills.

2. Worked as a stockbroker.

3. The servants were hidden.

4. Good reports or sports trophies.

5. "Good-bye, you little thug."

6. A Jewish girl.

7. Jewish.

8. "Mod Squad."

9. The Slackmeyers owned the original *Mayflower*.

10. They make such excellent caddies.

11. Marilou's fur coat.

12. Free Enterprise Seminar Training. An outreach program for the well-to-do run by John Connally.

13. Because they do such wonderful things with chicken.

14. The Council of Economic Advisors.

15. Invest in home furnishings, Chinese vases.

16. He couldn't live on just $62,000 a year.

17. Because everyone in his private booth was working and no one was having fun.

18. It now takes five martinis for a big business deal, six for a merger.

19. Trendex and Spanco.

20. Jim "Obscene Profits" Andrews.

21. Middle-aged Republican who drinks like a fish, enjoys making money, and detests all minority groups.

22. Somewhere along the line, the Slackmeyers' baby got mixed up with the Simpsons' boy.

23. His plummeting stock portfolio.

Politics

1. Watts.

2. At the Tomb of the Unknown Innocent Bystander.

3. A new era of peace between the L.A.P.D. and the hot young bucks.

4. As "a glorious safari."

5. "The Beverly Hillbillies."

6. Spiro Agnew.

7. "Okay, you snobs, the picnic's over!"

8. "Well, John, how's the cover-up going?"

9. A special update from "As the Hospital Turns."

10. Fritters, Alabama, Pop. 1,635, 95% employed, all white.

11. San Clemency.

12. "Richard Nixon's Secret Tapes Club Band!"

13. That it was none of their "damn" business.

14. By erecting a wall in front of the White House.

15. James Earl Carter.

16. The CIA and the Atlanta Braves.

17. Out back in the pond, hunting for frogs.

18. Three dollars a glass.

19. Guido "Sticky Fingers" Toglio, a colleague of Ray's from the construction business.

20. Tina Tibbit.

21. She worked on Congressman Phil Ventura's banking committee.

22. "We're at war with Japan, again."

23. He was in a key meeting with the ambassador from Iran.

24. The Golden Key Motel, Room 18.

25. She only did it for the Bicentennial.

26. "Congressman Meets In Love Nest For Nuke Recitations."

27. The text for the new nuclear test-ban treaty.

28. On-site inspections.

29. By yelling "Hey! Congressman!" in the motel-room window.

30. A plea for forgiveness and understanding.

31. Five poets, two ballet dancers, and a Nobel Prize laureate.

32. "He may be a moral cripple, but he's paid his debt to society" and "Don't forget! Hire the Watergate vet!"

33. Citizens for Phyllis George's Husband.

34. A racehorse.

35. Jackie liked sixteenth-century Florence, with its accent on the arts, but Ethel and the kids were favoring the Age of Pericles.

36. At least thirty-six hours. The paperwork is incredible.

B.D.

1. Brian John Dowling.

2. Maria.

3. He built F-100s before being laid off and becoming a janitor.

4. "Championship Bowling."

5. Poland.

6. Dancing school.

7. Sally Hudson.

8. ROTC boot camp.

9. Brownies.

10. Sears' mens department.

11. 800 million Communists.

12. Cooking sukiyaki.

13. To get out of writing a term paper.

14. "To the Nam!"

15.   George.

16.   Rice paddies.

17.   Firebase Bundy.

18.   Arnold, Seymour, or Peabody.

19.   A protective reaction strike means never having to say you're sorry.

20.   He cut himself on a beer-can tab.

21.   Phred.

22.   "How do you feel about the P.O.W. issue?"

23.   Phred's can of rice.

24.   Commies have mothers.

25.   A lousy commie gook.

26.   "Now doesn't that feel better?"

27.   Bob Hope.

28.   B.D. is the quarterback, with Calvin, Frank, Zonker, and Kirby in the backfield. Jonathan is the center. Also playing are Terry, Ron, Bill, John, Bruce, and Ralph.

29.   The sky opens and a dove with an olive branch in its beak flies out to the tune of the "Hallelujah Chorus."

30.   Number 10.

31.   Beneath the cool exterior of a huddle lurks the subtle dynamics of a nursery-school recess.

32.   As the Fellini of football.

33.   The Young Republicans Club.

34.   Breaking heads.

35.   The Dallas Cowboys.

36.   The Cincinnati Bengals.

37.   Amalgamated Shoulderpads Industries.

38.   Boopsie.

39.   Wet T-shirts.

40.   Communism.

41.   "He's as good a politician as he was an actor."

Boopsie

1. Barbara Ann Boopstein.

2. Mike Doonesbury. They went to the drugstore for a
    soda.

3. Exploited.

4. Tiger.

5. *Vogue* and *Cosmopolitan.*

6. Cheerleading.

7. *Playboy;* for $400.

8. Zonker.

9. A cowgirl.

10. Kurt Klieg.

11. "Girls of the Ivy League."

12. Four days and three nights doing Elvis.

13. The Elvis Presley Motor Lodge.

14. "Love Me Tender" came on the radio.

15. Three dozen white lilies shaped like a broken heart with a guitar in the center made of white carnations and a pink satin "Elvis Forever" sash.

16. An E-47 without the motor.

17. An exact miniature replica of Elvis' gravestone, with a little thermometer.

18. Two million necrophiliacs can't be wrong.

19. Both him and Lieutenant Shriver.

20. Prairie populist.

21. The farm animals, especially the baby ducks.

22. Jane Fonda.

23. Clinics to help migrant farmers meet their exercise needs.

24. While they have strong upper arms, they completely neglect those important abdominals.

Phred

1. As Phred the terrorist.

2. He can raze a hamlet in thirty seconds.

3. Nguyen Van Phred.

4. Hue, Vietnam.

5. Family tradition. His father had been a terrorist against the French.

6. He put in five years in a cadre outside of Ho Chi Minh City.

7. He once told a guy that he'd better stop supporting the tyrant Thieu or Phred would blow up his bicycle.

8. The Mekong Haberdashery.

9. Mort and Murray.

10. Chuck Berry, Elvis, and Cole Porter.

11. Running Dog.

12.   Schlitz beer.

13.   Gin rummy.

14.   He says that Phred is no commie-come-lately.

15.   With a twenty-one-mortar salute.

16.   The usual senseless terrorism, mostly.

17.   A Phord Phellowship.

18.   Leonid Brezhnev and Jane Fonda.

19.   The Pathet Lao.

20.   Phred had demanded better terms on the renewal of his ten-year terrorist contract.

21.   *The All-New Tommy Tourist Guide To Laos: 1961*.

22.   135,000.

23.   Cambodia.

24.   He ships them in crates on a plane flown by an expatriate Australian.

25.   200,000 empty Coca-Cola bottles.

26.   Three village elders and a war orphan.

27.   Senator Tunney.

28.   A Navy McDonnell F4B-1 Phantom II.

29. He taught Communism at the Vietnamese People's Reeducation Center for the Ministry of Education.

30. Their chains.

31. Lou Tho, Jr. and his dad, Lou Tho, Sr.

32. Marx and Engels.

33. He couldn't write for beans.

34. She was a former debutante and unimpressed by the *Manifesto*.

35. He got booted out for spying.

36. Two pinstripe suits, one linen blazer, seven silk shirts, four ties, three pleated trousers and two pair wing tips.

37. Victor Pinto from Benin.

38. By gross national product.

39. Eddie Kodjo.

40. First door on the left. Plowshares Lounge.

41. Benin, Vietnam, Malawi, Seychellis, Burundi, Lesotho, Bhutan, Mali, and of course, Upper Volta.

Uncle Duke I

1. Raoul Duke.

2. Zonker (though he is called Uncle Duke he is really jus
    an old friend of the family).

3. "Aunt" Sandy.

4. Muncie, Indiana.

5. He was a fireman.

6. 1963.

7. He's under his desk, killing bats with a ruler.

8. When he was local sewer commissioner in Colorado.

9. John Denver.

10. Five-hundred cases of Coors.

11. Lester.

12. Goebbels and Goering.

13. By putting land mines on the sofa.

14. Goebbels got rabies and Goering was shot by a deer hunter.

15. Zeke Brenner.

16. He starts to see huge, hairy bats.

17. Seventy-five micrograms of an extract made from the pineal glands of male adolescent iguanas.

18. It turned the Republicans into winged lizards and sheep.

19. .44 Colt Magnum.

20. *Rolling Stone*.

21. Yawn Wenner.

22. National Affairs Editor.

23. Fifteen-thousand words on snorkeling.

24. He became the governor of American Samoa.

25. Zonker Harris.

26. To stalk the perfect tan.

27. MacArthur.

28. Doug.

29. Hirohito.

30. The Battle of Midway.

31. A silver thermos full of daiquiris.

32. Release all political prisoners and burn all John Denver records.

33. By sacrificing virgins.

34. Two-thousand years.

35. Suzy Willowmaker.

36. She didn't do it because she had a dentist appointment.

37. Sacrificial virgin, Class of '62. Did a triple gainer on the way down.

38. They sacrificed a doubleheader.

39. Twelve math teachers.

40. Minister of Marijuana.

41. Six cases of Wild Turkey, 165 cases of Coors, 55 cases of Dom Perignon, 18 cases vodka, 25 gallons hearty Burgundy, and 23 cases of dry gin.

42. He has the cook flogged.

43. He wanted to invade Australia.

44. By declaring war and having MacArthur seize a luxury liner.

45. Operation Frequent Manhood.

46. Fiji, Tahiti, and Pago Pago.

47. Diplomacy.

48. The tuna cannery.

49. The hookers arrived.

50. A 21″ screen color TV in every pot.

51. James "Universal Petroleum" Andrews.

52. He reports Duke to the highest authority on the island, which is the governor, who also happens to be Duke.

53. Complete restoration of the executive mansion patio bar.

54. One dollar.

55. A pair of chopsticks (solid wood).

56. The first Polynesian welfare state.

57. Hack writer, presumed dead at 45.

58. "I've come to kill you."

59. The Cher Task Force.

60. The John Denver Bureau.

61. T. F. Bannon of Torts, Tartz, and Torque.

62. Yes, Helvetian Savings and Loan #51830.

63. Henry Kissinger.

64. His record showed he knew how to work with minorities.

65. "My Chinese hosts can suck an egg."

66. "I don't make any comments about his lack of motor

skills and he doesn't hassle me about my interest in stimulants.''

67. The fall of the government, basing his bets on wall propaganda posters.

68. Shanghai.

69. $150.

70. A Cartier watch from his mother, a pistol from Zonker, and his favorite alkaloid from his supplier, Maurice LeNez.

71. By shooting bottles off the Great Wall.

72. Thirty feet high, 20 feet wide, 1,500 miles long, and 60-degree inclines.

73. A new respiratory tent with his compliments.

74. He was tickled pinko.

75. *Song Of The Tiger.*

76. Automatic-weapons fire.

77. One of China's hottest new committees.

78. It was swiped.

79. Valium.

80. That's how they avoid belonging to it.

81. A little massage parlor with bowling lanes.

82. Shady Groves Farms, a hundred acres of apricots for laetrile.

83. Tony Placebo. It turns out to be a wasteland in the desert.

84. One IBM Selectric typewriter, one crate of fresh grapefruit, three cases of Wild Turkey, two albino typists, and one trampoline.

85. At a Swiss boarding school with Helga, the headmistress.

86. $3,000.

87. In unmarked tens and twenties, in advance.

88. He's an attorney, and president of the Washington Redskins. He was quite impressed with Duke's detailed knowledge of the new work being done with high-performance steroids.

89. Lava Lava Lenny, the Polynesian Panzer.

90. 390 pounds of steaming Samoan.

91. Zonker and B.D.'s college team.

92. The Detroit Lions.

93. By feeding him a pineapple after every tackle.

94. He wanted his own universal set and his own meat locker.

95. DKE (which is actually a fraternity).

96. The one that he played with a broken leg.

97.   Duke's assistant, who was also the Redskins owner's nephew.

98.   Chemical parity with the opposing team.

99.   By standing lookout.

100.   A couple hundred mgs. of Dexedrine.

101.   With a dart gun.

102.   Rick Redfern.

103.   Cheeseburgers.

104.   He wanted Rick to accidentally start a fire with his peach flambé dessert so that he could slip out undetected.

105.   Eddie, the linebacker that Duke medicated and is now in a full-body cast.

106.   On a field trip to the frontal lobes.

107.   He was on the run after having shot it out with U.S. Marshals upon being fired from the Redskins.

108.   Room 402 of the Miami Ramada Inn.

109.   An overturned golf cart.

110.   It should have been scrapped years ago.

111.   Springfield.

112.   If Duke would testify before the Judiciary Committee hearings on gun control, the NRA would get Duke's

charges dropped, as well as suing the Redskins on Duke's behalf.

113. A widow who wasted nine muggers.

114. Dental records.

115. James "Obscene Profits" Andrews.

116. Commit an unspeakably depraved but highly patriotic act. He was supposed to bring in some bribe money that would free the Iranian oil fields.

117. Ten-thousand dollars and ten percent of the take, so long as he didn't have to work with Albanians, children, or pets.

118. Code name: Dipstick.

119. Eagle.

120. Mother.

121. $250,000.

Honey

1. Ms. Ching Huan.

2. Cher.

3. The Peking Chorale's *Indignantly Condemn The Wang-Chan-Chiang-Yao Gang Of Four.*

4. "Everyone Is Rejoicing Over The Wiping Out Of The Four Pests."

5. Chairman Mao.

6. The chaperone for Duke and Honey.

7. A polka-dot tie.

8. As an exchange student at Georgetown U.

9. Henry Kissinger's.

10. It's sort of a female social-action cadre.

11. How many panty raids per semester a house got.

12. Pizza.

13. Her government wanted their money's worth.

14. The native Americans (Redskins).

15. The soft underbelly of Washington nightclub life.

16. To testify at the Gang of Four trial.

17. An ex-busboy in a restaurant near Canton.

18. He was a vice-premier.

19. Thirty-five.

20. The killings were actually 34,375 unrelated acts of passion.

21. The five cockroaches had already been executed.

22. Same as the American dream, but without the mortgage payments.

Zeke Brenner

1. His fingernails.

2. Libra.

3. J. J. Caucus.

4. *Duke: Portrait of a Mentor.*

5. Bantam Books.

6. First person plural, like Barbara Walters' book.

7. Popeye Malone, a ghostwriter.

8. Hardcover or quick and dirty?

9. Adjectives, adverbs, that sort of thing.

10. Read the book.

11. Donahue, Dinah, and Cavett.

12. A windmill.

13. Turn it into a souvenir shop.

14. Zonker and Zeke, along with a gang of creditors, a couple of IRS guys, and a U.S. Marshal.

15. Green. He couldn't find a yellow one.

16. Lieutenant O'Malley.

Quotes I

1. Henry Kissinger in response to a question from his class.

2. Prof. Charlie Green, campus guru, laying some wisdom on Mark and Mike.

3. Virginia Slade to Joanie Caucus about Clyde.

4. Duke to Zonker when assigning him to cover Gregg Allman.

5. Bob Dylan to Jimmy Thudpucker about Dylan's music.

6. Clyde to Ginny and Joanie when they were encouraging Jenny Thudpucker's labor over the phone.

7. Gov. Jerry Brown as quoted by Rick Redfern to Duane Delacourt.

8. William F. Buckley.

Zonker Harris

1. Edgar.

2. Laurel Canyon, California.

3. Cornell.

4. He used to commute.

5. Three years.

6. He was a nationally known pervert.

7. Daniel Ellsberg, a Kink, and a pair of Pips.

8. Some monster bubble gum cards, three long letters from his draft board, his yearly correspondence from summer camp, and one pack grape Kool-Aid.

9. Zonker put their value at $135,000.

10. By getting rid of tuition.

11. That he may actually graduate and have to get a job.

12. At the movies.

13. Moonies and winos.

14. He got a University grant to spend spring vacation in Southeast Asia doing work for the campus paper.

15. Left quarterback.

16. Uptight end.

17. That the post office was in charge of registration.

18. Tanning.

19. His plants.

20. Drat!

21. Heewack!

22. The Lone Ranger.

23. First she nominated Zonker as a "favorite son" candidate, but then switched to McCloskey.

24. To send out for some pizza.

25. UCLA, Class of 1939.

26. His mother's TM instructor had put the moves on her.

27. Thirty-two years.

28. It was just his mom's way of getting out of the house.

29. Bartender, postman, deejay, reporter, and lieutenant governor.

30. He would open the mail and censor it for his customers.

31. Scotch on the rocks.

32.   Alice P. Schwartzman.

33.   The Princess Ten-Pins Bowling Ball, the lightweight model for dames.

34.   He had achieved the perfect tan.

35.   Gold-medal swimmer Mark Spitz.

36.   Frank Lucas, first-degree murder.

37.   Claude.

38.   Three seeds in the bottom of his luggage.

39.   It's thrown out due to the illegal bugging of Z's hotel room.

40.   Some sort of clothes designer.

41.   His parents never allowed him to strut his stuff, and he was afraid that the strobe lights would dry out his skin.

42.   Liza Minnelli and Bianca Jagger.

43.   Halston.

44.   Nathaniel Harris, Revolutionary War hero.

45.   One unflunkable ceramics course.

46.   General Dynamics, Northrup, IBM, and Westinghouse.

47.   A life spent in search of the perfect hash brownie.

48.   "Singing in the Rain."

Nate Harris

1. He was a fast dresser and he loved firearms.

2. Amy Harris.

3. She wanted to become a minuteperson.

4. Paul Revere as an apprentice silversmith.

5. She negotiated it down to six years with four pregnancy leaves, but only because Nate was a Catholic.

6. Friend of Paul's (writes real big!).

7. Massachusetts.

8. Joshua.

9. Sammy Tucker.

10. Virginia.

11. The wording was pretty ambiguous.

12. Crouching behind stone walls.

13. They were fit to be tied.

14.   A slave.

15.   Assemble freely, bear arms, etc.

Plant Life

1. Wheat.

2. Explosives.

3. Ralph   Ed   George   Gertie
   Jack and Aretha   Willy   Chico   Zach
   Rob the Daffodil   Nemo the Begonia
   Fred the Perennial   Patty the Potted Palm

4. Chocolate compost cake.

5. A young blade's thoughts turn to pollen.

6. Recite "Gunga Din."

7. Walter Cronkite.

8. To a houseplant convention in Hartford, Conn.

9. D. Sanderiana from Essex.

10. An award-winning documentary on one day in the life of the sun, including some very controversial footage on dawn.

11. He was tired of being in the bush leagues.

12. Accuse Mike of killing him.

13.   B. J. Eddy.

14.   Eight years, until he was axed by the Carter transition
      team.

15.   The East Lawn.

16.   He was a perennial's perennial.

17.   Extra-terrarium.

Tanning

1. The George Hamilton Coppertone Pro-Am Cocoa Butter Open.

2. Photosynthesis.

3. Oakland. Malibu and Big Sur were booked solid.

4. Governor Brown and Proposition 13.

5. The small-car loan program for minority motorists.

6. Studio 54.

7. George gets many of his grad-votes on TV.

8. The Gerald R. Ford Summer Biathlon of tanning and golf.

9. Peelers.

10. Bernie.

11. *The Coppertone Guide to Great Tans of the Southwest.*

12. "Freeway Bold," Sonny Bono's old tan.

13. 255. The tan metered out at 16 and he shot 239 for 18 holes.

14. His perfect tan earned him the Jack Ford medal for Best Tan.

15. Bucky, Johnny, Skippy, Kenny, Barbie, Bunny, and P.J.

16. "The Hollywood Squares."

17. The parent company of Coppertone, in which Zonker has invested all of his money.

18. To devote his full time to his academic studies.

19. Absolutely no one.

20. An investigative reporter for *Tanning World* magazine.

Jimmy Thudpucker

1. Jenny.

2. She was running for state legislature.

3. Bob and Feedback or Bill and Rimshot.

4. *Roots*.

5. A psychiatric intern.

6. On the porch at Bob Dylan's house.

7. In the Jacuzzi, take a message.

8. He has to. It's in his contract.

9. Having his appendix out.

10. "Ginny's Song" for Virginia Slade's campaign.

11. A good rock tune with a nice melody and some catchy lyrics about her strong positions on busing and abortion. It also had to be a number one hit.

12. Dennis Parker, Pooh, and Jay "Wah Wah" Graydon.

13. It was so easy he could cut the record by mail.

14.   A disco version.

15.   Steve.

16.   Renee.

17.   He calls Stamp Mart and orders complete sets.

18.   Monaco and the Netherlands.

19.   Arizona Congressman Morris Udall.

20.   6,547,312.

A Doonesbury Special

1. John and Faith Hubley.

2. John was one of Garry Trudeau's teachers at Yale.

3. He had worked at the Disney studios on such films as *Snow White*, *Pinocchio*, and *Fantasia*.

4. The unfortunate passing of John Hubley in February, 1977.

5. NBC.

6. McAfee, the football player. "If only he had kept his head up."

7. Bernie and Nichole.

8. Ellie, Howie, and Jeanie.

9. He is hit by a National Guardsman's nightstick when he tries to help the Guard at a student demonstration.

10. Directing the Christmas rock pageant.

11. A 40-watt bulb.

12. "Stop in the Middle" and "I Do Believe."

Real People

1. Campus activist Mark Zanger.

2. Gonzo journalist Hunter S. Thompson.

3. New Jersey Congresswoman Millicent Fenwick.

4. The Reverend William Sloane Coffin, Jr.

5. Yale football star Brian Dowling.

6. Washington Post reporters Carl Bernstein and Bob Woodward.

7. Yale's president Kingman Brewster.

8. Actually the name of Garry Trudeau's good friend and editor at the Universal Press Syndicate.

Roland Burton Hedley, Junior

1. "The State of the Student" essay.

2. *Time*.

3. "The New Hedonism."

4. Zonker and the Walden gang.

5. Blue jeans allowed.

6. Peyote and clam dip.

7. Sports.

8. Harvard.

9. *Newsweek*.

10. Erich Lipsett.

11. Mostly hypothetical.

12. The Friends of Exxon society.

13. Star Quality.

14. The voice-over. It saves time.

15. Rollie's report on the Camp David summit meetings.

16. An inadmissibly occupied territory.

17. The land of milk and honey.

18. As peace ravaged.

19. Ted Kennedy.

20. ABC TV's ".30/.30."

21. "Beats me. I thought we had the suckers under control."

22. "Lavishly, without hesitation."

23. Henry Kissinger's book *The White Wash Years*.

24. By almost any standard, *White Wash Years* is a very big book.

25. "Have you been to Studio 54 yet?"

26. 1931.

27. 1944.

28. Anacin.

29. "One for the Gipper."

30. A good pair of underwear.

31. To keep Rollie out of his hair.

32. The Hotel Commodore.

33. Five.

34.   Five-dollar deposit on hotel bath towels.

35.   He went unshaven, clad in the indigenous garb of an
      Afghan mountaineer, to investigate the Soviet-Afghanistan
      border fighting.

36.   Life goes on.

Duane Delacourt

1. Symbolism.

2. Sheila.

3. James Earl Carter.

4. Secretary of Symbolism.

5. No pay-raise.

6. It was a victory for the "little guy," the average Joe.

7. The call-in show, the fireside chat, the cardigan sweater, the limo cuts, full financial disclosure, Amy's trustee governess, and the Human Rights Banquet.

8. Telethons that allowed average Americans to call in and say what symbols they'd most like to see.

9. Brazil.

10. Guinea.

11. Nicaragua.

12. It was a nine-way tie for Western Europe.

13. Alexander Haig.

14.   The James Earl Carter Atonement Cup.

15.   A little guy struggling with his chains and an inscription from Gandhi.

16.   Blue jeans; a three-piece suit.

17.   It was a chance to work with some of the most important rhetorical questions of our time.

18.   Carter was trying to address the issues, without symbols.

19.   Spaceship Earth.

20.   Californian or Mellowspeak.

21.   Moonrock.

22.   "My beliefs and my convictions are what the people choose to project on me. I see no need for any of my own."

23.   By divorcing. Their relationship wasn't shallow enough.

24.   The new Walter Mondale.

25.   Neo-nice—niceness with a liberal face.

Events from the Headlines

1. In the White House swimming pool.

2. Snow Bunny.

3. Ford's Moviegoer's Assistance Program.

4. William E. Simon.

5. Your Exchequership.

6. Hot wax and a signet ring.

7. The American couple who adopted Kim, the last orphan to come out of Vietnam.

8. "Big Mac."

9. "Hold the pickle."

10. Scot, Scot, and Ted.

11. The lieutenant governor of Iowa.

12. None.

13. He couldn't get any coverage from the N.Y. *Daily News*.

14. They finally nailed him through his clipping service.

15. The worst media blitz in recent history. It was about the G.O.P. caucus being held there.

16. Dummy warheads at three for $50,000.

17. Half a trillion dollars.

18. "Nine? Y'all play softballs?"

19. An undercover operation led by seven congressmen and a senator to investigate entrapment rings being run by the FBI.

20. A mobster from whom Jerry Brown reportedly accepted a bribe.

21. "Gregg was so thoughtful. He stayed off drugs the whole afternoon."

22. Gold.

23. Because all the good names, like God, China, Free, and America, were already taken.

24. "Splits."

25. Eighty-three.

26. Dancing bears and jugglers.

27. *Weed's Eye View.*

28. Mr. Weed, Steverino, and Insect, each at different times in their relationship.

29. "A tiny little thing with very pretty mother-of-pearl inlay and little daisies etched on the barrel."

30. Teeny-weeny bullets.

31. The head of a Trojan horse.

32. Ralph Edwards offered him a copy of Machiavelli's *The Prince*.

33. She was always reminded of the many children who were maimed and killed during the Christmas bombing of Bach Mai Hospital.

34. Modesty.

35. Operation Manhood.

Rick Redfern

1. Rathbone.

2. The "indiscretion" of Congressman Phil Ventura.

3. The Washington *Post*.

4. Rollo.

5. The New York *Tribune*.

6. Stamps editor.

7. Virginia Slade's congressional campaign.

8. Truth, beauty.

9. "We're getting absolutely nowhere." He used it for the campaign; she meant their love life.

10. They're in his house.

11. TV dinners and Dr. Pepper.

12. *People*.

13. That Rick wouldn't have to cover Marisa Berenson and that he could leave in six months.

14. People Seminar Training, a symposium on personality journalism.

15. The Jackie O. retrospective.

16. Edmund Muskie's Melting Snowflake.

17. Like waking up in Bridgeport, only ten times worse.

18. Be debriefed on the Fonz.

19. The world needs grown-ups.

20. An egg-salad sandwich.

21. Due to a triple high in his biorhythms.

22. The Zoo Plane.

23. Riley, Duke's assistant.

24. "Drug Doc Termed Menace To Sports."

25. A writer who came to interview Rick for a book about the giants of journalism.

26. *La Creme de la Creme*.

27. *The Powers That Be* and *The Best and The Brightest*.

28. Brut.

29. A Rorschach test.

30. "Brown Assembles Mellow Mafia."

31. From over 10,000 clippings dating back to the 1930s that Reagan was carrying around in shoeboxes.

32. Ted Simpson.

33. Mrs. Gorsuch, The Ice Queen.

34. Getting ready to jump off the ledge.

35. To show he had clout.

36. Panda matings.

37. Mixed them all together in the same drawer.

38. Mononucleosis.

Joanie Caucus Redfern

1. Cleveland.

2. Clinton Caucus.

3. Played a pleading tape recording of their daughter's voice.

4. She broke his nose.

5. Clint wore his bowling shoes to see her off.

6. July 21, 1935.

7. Louisa.

8. July 21, 1972. (Happy Birthday!)

9. Roast beef.

10. Walden Day Care Center.

11. 760.

12. Berkeley, Georgetown, Boston University, and Harvard.

13. The University of California at Berkeley.

14. Virginia Slade.

15. Fifty dollars a month; twenty-five more if Joanie wanted to cohabitate.

16. Andrew Lippincott.

17. Andy had reserved a library copy of *Top Torts* that Joanie needed.

18. After dating a bit, Andy admitted he was gay.

19. That he was cheerful.

20. He was an organizer of the Bay Area Gay Alliance in Lacey Davenport's district.

21. Woodrow.

22. Professor Lathrop's.

23. Rick Redfern.

24. A few years later, she would give him a confidential committee file on one of the key figures in the Koreagate investigation.

25. Lacey Davenport.

26. The House committee investigating Koreagate.

27. $22,000.

28. Good old Woodrow.

29. $28,000.

30. No. Congress is perfectly free to discriminate on the basis of race, sex, or color of socks.

31. That she isn't independently wealthy.

32. Joanie's butcher.

33. Due to a computer error.

34. The guilty make much better television.

35. An award given when one presses their investigation with such integrity and vigor that they end up getting fired.

36. Because Prince Charles and Lady Diana were getting married on the twenty-ninth. Better to avoid comparisons.

37. Bick Redfern.

38. Bridegoon.

39. June 18, 1981, 3:00 P.M. at 312 Foxhunt Road, Washington, D.C.

40. Zonker. He said that they hadn't known each other long enough.

41. Four years.

42. Probably the night the dishwasher broke down.

43. Dr. Phipps.

44. A boy with sandy hair, freckles, and an aptitude for math. He would also be a Red Sox fan.

J.J.

1. Joanie's daughter, Joan Jr.

2. Seven years.

3. Seventeen.

4. Madison Grammar.

5. For smoking dope on the school bus.

6. Unsalted nuts.

7. Zeke Brenner.

8. He burned down the house they were staying at in Aspen.

9. Joan Sr. brought Mike home to sleep over after an Anderson fund-raiser hosted by Lacey Davenport.

10. A nerd.

11. When she found out that Mike was one of the motorcycle guys who picked up her mother.

12. Better dope.

13. To a movie and then to a Randy Newman concert, from 8:00 to 11:00 on Mike's schedule.

14. A restaurant that Mike and J.J. go to in Washington.

15. Honey, Duke's Chinese flame.

The Kids Are All Right

1. Howie and Ellie were the mainstays, with support coming from Jeanie, Sally, Jenny, Tommy, Lisa, Mary, Nina, Lilly, Cathy, Chickadee, et al.

2. Boys.

3. A baby woman.

4. He has a tendency to withdraw.

5. Walden Center's token holdover. His mother still wears granny dresses and his father's into candles.

6. Ms. Latour.

7. Miss MacGregor.

8. Billie Jean King, of course.

9. 11,000.

10. In order to campaign for the ratification of the ERA.

11. Because it was boring.

12. Through the use of coupons.

13. A wristwatch.

14. Busing. It was the note Bobby's mother gave him to hand blacks.

15. A black 7-year-old bussee. He was Bobby's partner in fear.

16. Joe.

17. Honky.

18. Batman comics.

19. Sergeant DeRosa.

20. Ricky.

Virginia Slade

1. Congressperson.

2. As a seminar project for school.

3. The incumbent, Phil Ventura, as well as Lacey Davenport.

4. 7:00 P.M.

5. 4:30, but she had a pottery class and had to shop for dinner.

6. There was nowhere near enough lead time.

7. Zonker Harris.

8. He watched about five hours a day.

9. Andy Lippincott (which made things tough for Joanie).

10. Four percent.

11. A hot tub and a nice book.

12. Clyde.

13. Four months.

14.   Move in with Ginny.

15.   His toothbrush, in case of an opening.

16.   Santa Claus.

17.   A sky-blue Electra 225 with the baddest V-8 ever to leave Detroit, with an eight-track tape deck, silver fox fur seats, and a chrome stallion on the hood. Just $6,000.

18.   Free cheeseburgers for the elderly.

19.   The Ninth.

20.   Because they had more hardcore bigots than Rhodesia.

21.   A Woolco tie.

22.   Ol' Man Munson.

23.   Mrs. Pocatelli.

Lacey and Dick Davenport

1. She's a proud member of the Grand Old Party.

2. Donate it to the Department of Health, Education, and Welfare.

3. She won by the biggest margin in the state.

4. Handguns and oil.

5. "With apologies from the New Jersey mob." This was after they realized their mistake.

6. A small media event.

7. Senator and Mrs. Elizabeth Taylor.

8. Only to wait outside in the car.

9. Eating their way across France.

10. Thirty-five years.

11. The pressure from Lacey's parents was unbelievable.

12. Yes. She was once mad for the entire Yale crew of 1927.

13. Dick went right out and got a job clerking in Boston, Lacey stayed on to get her law degree.

14. At one of the early reunions Mark was bartending.

15. They roomed together at summer camp in 1913.

16. Pale blue. Not violet, sorry.

17. Navy.

18. He's an ornithologist with the Maryland Audubon Society.

19. The Bachman Warbler.

20. A society of those who've seen seven hundred or more North American birds.

21. Thadius.

22. He became extinct.

23. The Beak. Even then they knew he would be a birdwatcher.

24. Yes. Dick's Uncle Orville, who's a federal judge in Chicago.

25. "Because he doesn't stand a chance."

26. Vacuous baritones.

27. "The most bizarre collection of cronies, retreads, and tokens ever assembled."

28.   No, because Watt was appointed on a Wednesday when Reagan was out horseback-riding.

29.   Rape.

30.   All the caddies.

The Brother of M.J. Doonesbury

1. Benjamin P. Doonesbury ("Benjy" to his friends).

2. Harvard Medical.

3. Over four hundred.

4. January 1 of his third-grade year.

5. He wanted to be a doctor so he and his classmates could open a clinic in Southampton, make 5 or 6 million dollars, and then retire and start a commune in Barbados.

6. To make lots of money.

7. Marrying a beautiful student nurse from Chicago.

8. Lana Turner, "The Sweater."

9. Sal Putrid.

10. Saliva.

11. To go to Berlin, work the punk clubs, and live in a squatters house with German skinheads until he gets a record contract.

Rufus Jackson

1. A dumb honky.

2. He was paid for it.

3. Thor.

4. A nuclear physicist or the leader of a puppet government.

5. The Gold Coast.

6. Diane.

7. The Philistines.

8. A #3 orange pencil.

9. Joseph.

10. A Nubian slave.

11. A mourning cloak.

12. Afro-American Day.

13. Fresh pâté de fois, artichoke hearts au beure, and a

seasoned fillet garnished with petit pois and a light Chablis '62.

14. Positively Baroque.

15. He would be forced to put up with all of the "uppity black folk."

Quotes II

1. Some factory worker, in answer to a Chinese contest.

2. Alexander Haig to Ronald Reagan on whether the U.S. could deliver a nuclear warning shot.

3. Elizabeth Taylor supporting John Warner.

4. Mark to Mike on the plane to Washington for a protest rally.

5. Former President Gerald Ford.

6. Virginia State Senator Wiley Mitchell about putting a censure on "Doonesbury" because of the John Warner strips.

7. Art Buchwald.

8. Popular Maoist saying that sums up the Chinese position in regard to dealing with Russia.

Fin de Decade Party

1. Steven Weed.

2. OPEC.

3. As labels on Perrier bottles.

4. A staggering deficit.

5. The 1975 Pittsburgh Steelers.

6. They were 12 and 2 that year.

7. Eddy.

8. A '50s revival, disco, and Watergate books. (Not to mention tomes of trivia.)

9. Zonker: "To a kidney stone of a decade."
   Mike: "To the worst of times."

Extras

1. Stepping fine and singing background in groups like the Pips.

2. To Cranston.

3. A restaurant in Washington, D.C.

4. Duke was appointed manager of the Redskins, Duke takes Honey to show her Washington, and Riley leaked the Redskins' drug problem to Rick Redfern. It didn't all happen at the same time, though.

5. There is a Zonker Harris Memorial Beach in Malibu that was approved by the California Coastal Commission.

6. He married a coed.

7. Mr. Smooth.

8. Walter Wooten.

9. The crippled housing industry.

10. They turned him on to Granola.

11. He was the most qualified to wing it.

12. His tankards.

13. Health reasons.

14. "Spa."

15. Full frontal nudity and chimps.

16. John Travolta and Suzanne Somers.

17. Congressman Thomas O'Neill, Washington, D.C.

18. "Yours for a clean Congress."

19. *People* magazine.

20. Shahs.

21. "God is great," (or more loosely, "We're number one.").

22. "Henry, please drop as many bombs on my country as were dropped on Japan in all of World War Two."

23. Jim Andrews got behind in his mail.

24. Katic.

25. A red neck.

Titles

1. Elizabeth Taylor, according to one of her own bumper stickers.

2. Ginny's comment on Clyde's car.

3. The final comment at the end of the senate investigation into Vietnam atrocities. Speidel watches were the first thing.

4. Joanie offering to spend the night with Rick Redfern.

5. Mike's comment to passersby as he's campaigning for John Anderson.

6. *Bravo for Life's Little Ironies*

7. *But the Pension Fund Was Just Sitting There*

8. *Guilty! Guilty! Guilty!*

9. *You Give Great Meeting, Sid*

10. *Speaking of Inalienable Rights*

11. William F. Buckley.

12. Jackson Browne.

13.   Walt Kelly, creator of "Pogo."

14.   Jim Andrews, editor and friend.

Uncle Duke II

1. A record of failure and malfeasance that spanned over twenty years.

2. Since 1963.

3. His protégé, Zonker.

4. The Bald Spy.

5. Ahmad and Asif.

6. Soccer games behind the compound, late nights of drinking, and a sailing vacation in Greece.

7. An extra $300.

8. The tendency of a hostage to sympathize with his tormentors.

9. His Former Hostage ID card, good for reductions of up to fifty percent.

10. Duke's caretaker, Zeke Brenner.

11. He set out to kill Brenner.

12. A department-store Santa Claus.

13.   Alice P. Schwartzman.

14.   The life story of John DeLorean.

15.   *Fast Lanes, White Lines*.

16.   Sid Kibitz.

17.   Dan Aykroyd.

18.   By selling dope (he winds up selling them to the FBI).

19.   A 2000-horsepower Cabin Cruiser with a cargo hold big enough to take fifty bales easily, complete with a deck gun.

20.   A guy named Rodriguez, for $2000.

21.   Rusty Nail Charters.

22.   Ship's purser.

23.   Diaz wanted Duke to pick up a package from the Caracan freighter *San Pedro*.

24. $35.00.

25.   The Coast Guard cutter *Nemesis*.

26.   Duke is supposed to go to Port-Au-Prince to pick up and smuggle in two hundred Haitian deep-sea fishermen.

27.   The fishermen are offered a better deal by another captain, and Duke is left with only one passenger.

28.   By telling Duke to think of this trip as a loss leader.

29.   Alphonse Petit-Pois.

30. After being picked up by police in the U.S., he is pressed into service as Duke's son and deckhand.

31. It gets shipwrecked on a sandbar where Duke and Honey are forced to live like savages.

32. A parrot.

33. In Vietnam.

34. A door.

35. The island of Matagorda, off the coast of Texas.

36. She lost them to Duke in a poker game.

37. Dick Davenport, while out bird-watching.

Doonesbury on Broadway

1. Graduation and the saving of Walden.

2. Mike, Mark, Duke, Zonker, Roland Burton Hedley, Jr., Boopsie, J.J., Joanie, Honey, B.D., the President.

3. The class of 1983.

4. Go to Europe for a summer.

5. B.D.

6. Football player.

7. Dallas Cowboys.

8. To go on to business school.

9. On trial for cocaine use/possession.

10. That he was conducting acquisitions of narcotics for the State Dept. under direct orders of George Shultz.

11. The jury.

12. Honey, due to her expert testimony.

13. State-of-the-art bullshit.

14. Guilty with probation, providing he establish and direct a drug rehabilitation center for no less than five years.

15. Walden Commune.

16. Mrs. Kirby.

17. Ralph, Laurel, Ginger, and Arnold the cactus.

18. Tanning.

19. Apply for a Fulbright scholarship.

20. It firms you up and expands your political consciousness at the same time.

21. Serious acting.

22. It's disgusting.

23. Because the women who supported it were always grossing everyone out, by doing things like breast-feeding, etc.

24. Jeffrey.

25. "I am woman, hear me hyperventilate."

26. 787-4311.

27. "Fred" Cronkite, "Mad Jack" Chancellor, and "Old Rag Head."

28. Domingo.

29. To marry him.

30. Supposedly, it's lasagna.

31. Duke busting into Walden with a spray of smoke, and ordering everyone else out.

32. The roar of Duke's bulldozer as it plows through the Walden meadow.

33. A red hard hat with a yellow star on it.

34. "Effete ACLU looney types."

35. Dexedrine, according to Honey.

36. The firepower of the local police force.

37. An AK-47.

38. Turn it into the priciest, most profitable vacation condo complex in New England.

39. Resident Tanning Director.

40. When Duke comes busting into the house at Walden on his bulldozer.

41. Bats wearing panty hose, and Helga the headmistress.

42. B.D.

43. Sid Kibitz.

44. The Tampa Bay Buccaneers.

45. Two draft choices and a bus.

46. "TV Wrestling."

47. Chocolate pancakes.

48. The Tampets.

49. Muffy and the Topsiders.

50. Feeds him Grapenuts and draws a mustache on his face.

51. "You're gonna love it!"

52. He gets a job as deejay on an "all-talk" station on Long Island.

53. Sheldon.

54. They ride over in Roland's limousine.

55. *Cum laude.*

56. "Mike, you weeny!"

57. Cum Granum Salis. (Welcome Big Salaries?)

58. He becomes comatosed.

59. Garry Trudeau.

60. Elizabeth Swados.

61. *Nightclub Cantata, Runaways, Alice in Concert, The Haggadah,* and her first novel, *Leah and Lazar.*

62. Mike's not wanting to rush J.J. into anything physical about their relationship. It's a touching song about taking things slowly and trying to develop a basis for a fuller relationship.

63. Duke's pleas to the jury. What he says he's guilty of is just caring too much and trying too hard.

64. Boopsie's coming of age and gaining new self-confidence.

65. J.J. and Mike finally getting a commitment going in their feelings for each other.

66. Mark's plea for a paying job at WBBY.

67. A reply by all to B.D.'s comment about Duke's taking over.

68. Honey and Boopsie singing about their respective mates.

69. Duke's trying to convince Zonker about the merits of condos. This song should actually be called "Mondo Condo."

70. J.J.'s reconciliation with Joanie.

71. B.D. and Rollie celebrating the good life with backup from Muffy and the Topsiders, an all-preppie group.

72. "Graduation" by the group; "I Came To Tan" by Zonker and his plants; and "Another Memorable Meal" by the group.

73. Roland Burton Hedley, Jr.

74. Zonker.

75. Duke.

76. Honey.

77. Mike Doonesbury.

78. J. J. Caucus.

79. Mark Slackmeyer.

80. B.D.

81. Boopsie.

82. Joanie Caucus.

83. The Biltmore on West 47th.

84. The Wilbur.

85. The show opened on November 21, 1983, and ran until February 19, 1984.

86. The provost, played by Peter Shawn.

87. A new scene where Ronald Reagan makes campaign commercials for the black vote and the Hispanic vote, a camera crew to cover the graduation ceremonies, and a costume change for Boopsie during "I Can Have It All" because the old costume showed the microphone.

88. Honey's testimony and dance with the Dream Duke, as well as the Dream Duke himself.

89. The Seattle Seahawks.

90. A Tiernecito Doll by Jesmar of Spain.

The Man Behind the Scenes

1. Garretson Beekman Trudeau.

2. New York City, 1948.

3. Two sisters, Michelle and Jeanne.

4. TV reporter and commentator Jane Pauley.

5. Yes, a set of twins.

6. Junk food and Dr. Pepper.

7. "Little Nemo."

8. "To Tell The Truth," yes.

9. Yale, starting in 1966.

10. Six years.

11. Fine Arts.

12. He was made a Doctor of Humane Letters in 1976,
    holds an honorary law degree from Berkeley, as well as
    degrees from Colgate, Williams and a dozen other
    colleges.

13. It was nominated for an Academy Award and won the Special Jury Prize at the Cannes Film Festival.

14. The Pulitzer Prize for editorial cartooning, the first regular strip to ever do so.

15. He supported a resolution to condemn the Pulitzer committee.

16. 1968, in *The Yale Daily News*.

17. "Bull Tales."

18. Long-time friend and editor, Jim Andrews.

19. January 2, 1983.

20. More than 700 worldwide.

21. 572.

22. Some of them supported the Connecticut Red Cross Blood Drive, and Joanie's face was used by the National Organization of Women.

23. New Haven, Connecticut.

24. The "Son of Arnold and Mary Leiberman" and the Joanie/Rick love affair.

25. Richard Nixon's trip to Watts.

26. John Mitchell's "Guilty, Guilty, Guilty," by Mark.

27. They all ran "Doonesbury" the comic strip on their editorial pages.

28. At least six different papers banned "The Search For Reagan's Brain."

29. He once hid in a men's room for four hours in order to avoid a reporter.

30. The excavation of a small medieval town.

31. Trudeau designed some murals for Lindsay's Ping-Pong room at Gracie Mansion.

32. A columnist for the Washington *Post*.

33. "Tales From The Margaret Mead Taproom" and "The Fireside Watergate."

34. Don Vito Corleone.